Praise

'Penny Hopkinson "gets" franchising. *Manual Magic* is a must-have book for any franchisor. If you are a franchisor, read this book. It will help you identify the flaws in your current Operations Manual. If you are planning to franchise your business, read this book. You will use it as a template to provide your franchisees with the best possible companion on their franchise journey.

'I've been involved in franchising for 17 years. This is the most important book I've read. It will help any franchisor set the right tone with their franchisees.'

— **Steve Ennis**, BFA Franchise Champion

'Penny's *Manual Magic* brilliantly deconstructs the process of creating an impactful and practical Operations Manual. Her three-step process is a great approach and equips franchisees with a useable framework to successfully emulate the franchisor's Business System and achieve efficient growth. 100% recommended.'

— **Simon Hedley FCA**, Strategic Alchemist

'While working on The Eden Project system and Operations Manuals, I have found the 3-step principles in *Manual Magic* to be incredibly valuable. These principles have been successfully applied with multiple clients at Whitbread and in Java Group – East Africa. They have proven to be a great

support for developing first Operations Manuals and upgrading current ones. The process ensures relevant and engaging content, as well as cross-functional collaboration. I highly recommend *Manual Magic* as a must-read and great reference tool.'
— **Joanna K Dawson**, Consultant & Coach

'It's a treasure trove. So much knowledge and information to incorporate. And, on top of that, making it readable.'
— **Sheryll Webb**, HR Professional

'From not knowing where to start and everyone perceiving it as a chore, creating our AA Driving School Manual became a pleasure. It was very satisfying and rewarding because of the simple method Penny has developed and how the AA brand was represented throughout.'
— **Gill Balshaw**, former Head of
The AA Training Academy

MANUAL *Magic*

Create the operations manual your franchisees need to succeed

PENNY HOPKINSON

Re think

First published in Great Britain in 2023
by Rethink Press (www.rethinkpress.com)

*This book is dedicated to the franchise community –
the entrepreneurs, clients, professional advisors and
other colleagues – without whom my 40-year career in
franchising would not have been so enjoyable, and this
book would not have been possible.*

Contents

Foreword

A s a franchisor, you have worked tirelessly to bring your brand to market, launch a franchise and grow your network. You have accumulated years of knowledge, have fine-tuned your business, and have undoubtedly made mistakes along the way. But how do you successfully capture that know-how and transfer it to your network, ensuring that your systems and procedures are followed and that your franchisees operate profitable businesses?

I have been part of the franchise industry for over 23 years. Today, I am proud to lead the British Franchise Association (bfa), the UK's longest-established and largest not-for-profit association for franchising. The bfa is built around its standards with a core aim to support and influence high-quality, ethical business format franchising. A key factor for anyone looking to invest in a franchise is to ensure they buy into an ethical business that is proven and genuinely transferable. While the franchisee is the company's owner, it is the franchisor's system and brand under which the franchisee is operating.

The franchise agreement will always form the legal backbone of the relationship between the franchisor and the franchisee, but the Operations Manual takes its rightful place as the essential guide that sets out how the business must be run so that the model can be successfully replicated. The manual is a process; you cannot have a successful franchise business without one. It is one of the essential tools for launching a franchise. Alongside comprehensive training, it forms a fundamental part of your franchise network's ongoing support and development.

Although businesses may operate in the same sector, every business is unique along with its system and processes. Two hairdressing or signage franchises may offer the same services, but their Unique Selling Proposition – the essence of what makes their product or service better than your competitors – will differ from their key messages. Also, a business should never stand still. It needs to evolve continuously, so there will be no single template you can take off the shelf and apply to your Operations Manual. In other words, one size will not fit all. As well as capturing everything a franchisee needs to know about setting up and running their franchise, in parallel to the business, the

Operations Manual will constantly evolve as the brand and network develop and grow. Producing a concise manual is not a one-off task. A good, well-maintained manual will be kept fresh and relevant, reflecting any amendments or modifications to the Business System.

I have worked closely with many brands – large and small – and have witnessed first-hand the evolution of the Operations Manual from a traditional typed, hard copy document into a powerful, fully integrated online tool that drives forward innovation in franchising. What is abundantly apparent is that getting it right is not easy. Many franchisors struggle to take their experience and what they do day-to-day and turn it into detailed, well-constructed procedures that cement the franchisor and franchisee obligations and protect the franchisor's brand and Intellectual Property. This is where an expert can be an invaluable resource. When it comes to developing a unique structure for *your* business and *your* Operations Manual, you will need to ensure that the content faithfully represents and transfers your know-how and Business System so that it's not left to your franchisees to interpret how to run your business their way.

I have known Penny for many years. She was one of the first Affiliate members to join the bfa in 1989. She worked closely with us to update our Franchisor and Franchisee Guides and, subsequently, edited our interpretation and extension of the European Code of Ethics. In 2011, she was deservedly appointed a Companion of the Association for her outstanding contribution to franchising. There is no doubt that Penny is a well-known and respected figure in our sector. Her sole focus and passion have always been to help franchisors produce professional Operations Manuals that help change their franchisees' lives and enable them to operate successful and profitable businesses. It is something she has championed throughout her career – one that spans more than 40 years – and has seen her work with some of the most prominent household names in the UK and internationally.

Now, Penny has poured her vast specialist knowledge into this book which will help you delve into your franchise business and take you through each stage of creating your Operations Manual, ensuring you are getting it right from the outset. Covering each process step in detail and using an illustrative case study to bring that process to life is your essential guide to producing and maintaining a comprehensive, consistent, and professional franchise Operations Manual.

Encapsulating everything from why you should have a manual, to how to structure it and build your content through to publication, it is a must-read whether you are new to franchising and preparing to launch or are an established brand with a developed network.

Pip Wilkins QFP
CEO, British Franchise Association
www.thebfa.org

Introduction

An expertly written Operations Manual is funda-mental for helping your franchisees grow and expand their businesses by providing them with the knowledge, guidance and support they need to succeed. However, if you want to write an Operations Manual that faithfully replicates your Business System, engages your franchise teams and makes them more efficient, you may need to rethink your entire approach to planning and creating your manual.

Manual Magic is a flexible and customisable formula allowing both new and mature franchisors to tailor content to their specific needs and goals to construct or upgrade their Operations Manual. The three parts of the book mirror the three steps of the Operations Manual creation process:

- Part One: Developing a sound structure.

- Part Two: Developing content.

- Part Three: Drafting to publication.

Using a unique approach developed during 35 years of working directly with sole traders, SMEs, multinationals and social enterprises, I will show you exactly how to structure your manual, what to cover and how to underpin the terms and conditions of the franchise agreement.

I explode the myth that all procedure manuals need to be dull, text-heavy tomes that nobody reads. I will reveal how you can create an engaging knowledge-sharing environment in which all team members can participate, learn and grow – one that you can scale as your franchise matures.

The Manual Magic system:

- Breaks down the process of creating an Operations Manual into manageable tasks, making the development process easier, more enjoyable and more satisfying.

- Helps you sift, organise and streamline your Intellectual Property (IP).

- Shows you how to create engaging content in less time than it takes to write text-only content.

- Identifies the best methods for knowledge sharing.

- Provides options for easily updating and upgrading your manual as you scale the business.

This will enable your franchises to faithfully replicate your Business System and gain a competitive advantage over other businesses in your sector.

Numerous books have been written on how to franchise a business or choose a franchise. However, until now, no one has written the definitive book on the Operations Manual – the most important tool after the franchise agreement.

A practical, effective Operations Manual that embodies the MAGIC principles below will support franchisees in achieving success, ensuring the growth and prosperity of the entire franchise network:

- **M**astering the franchise system: The Operations Manual provides franchisees with the knowledge and guidance they need to replicate the franchisor's proven Business System effectively. This helps maintain quality and consistency across the network. It builds a strong foundation for the success of each franchise.

- Achieving consistent brand standards: By defining the franchisor's expectations and guidelines for maintaining brand standards, the Operations Manual helps franchisees deliver a consistent customer experience. This consistency strengthens the brand's reputation and fosters customer loyalty.

- Generating profits: A comprehensive Operations Manual equips franchisees with the tools and strategies they need to maximise profitability. It includes best practices, proven sales techniques and operational efficiencies that help franchisees optimise their business performance.

- Implementing best practices: The Operations Manual holds invaluable information from the franchisor's extensive experience and industry expertise. By following recommended best practice, franchisees can confidently avoid common pitfalls and accelerate their path to success.

- Complying with all business processes and policies: A thorough Operations Manual provides detailed instructions on every aspect of franchise operations: from recruitment to marketing, customer service to day-to-day routines, and business development to the sale of the business. This comprehensive coverage ensures franchisees have easy access to the information they need to manage their business effectively.

Innovative technologies and Artificial Intelligence (AI) products help us to create manuals more quickly and effectively. The subject of AI is immense and continuously evolving. AI-enabled products such as ChatGPT from OpenAI allow us to cut development time dramatically. We can present content in a more engaging and versatile way than we ever thought possible. We can check the number of user interactions for individual instructions and evaluate what's working and what's not. We can update content in real time.

As we delve into how to create your MAGIC manual, we bring this to life through the illustrative Patisserie Pénélope case study. I created this fictional franchise for my individual and group workshops. Baking is the perfect metaphor for how to turn the Manual Magic recipe into a successful Operations Manual.

manualmagic.manual.to/**library**

Use your smartphone camera, capture the *Manual Magic* Library QR code and unlock additional tools and resources to help you develop your Operations Manual. This includes two real-life case histories describing how we developed the Costa

Coffee Operational Manual and the AA & BSM Driving School Manual. Both were instrumental in developing my three-step process.

You'll read about other franchisors' experiences, together with opinions from other experts in franchising. Jo Middleton, franchise mentor, says:

> 'Pretend I gave you a book and told you that it was a magic book. Everyone who reads it and acts develops an income stream – a regular money supply from their business. This book's successful formula has been proven time and time again. You'd read the book, right?
>
> 'This is what the Franchise Operations Manual is. It may not hold supernatural powers or cast charms and spells, but it does hold immense power – the power to make the impossible possible, so that people who want to run their own business but don't want to do it alone can run a successful and profitable franchise with first-rate support from their franchisor – and the magic book.'

By following the principles and strategies outlined in this book, you'll be able to create your own 'magic book' – one that honours the passion and dedication that inspired your franchise.

PART ONE

DEVELOPING A SOUND STRUCTURE: THE PERFECT BALANCE OF INGREDIENTS

Just as a chocolate brownie recipe requires specific measurements and steps to ensure the perfect balance of ingredients and texture, effective communication needs structure to ensure perfect information and delivery. Without a straightforward recipe or structure, the communication (or brownie) may turn out too dry, too gooey or not at all what was intended.

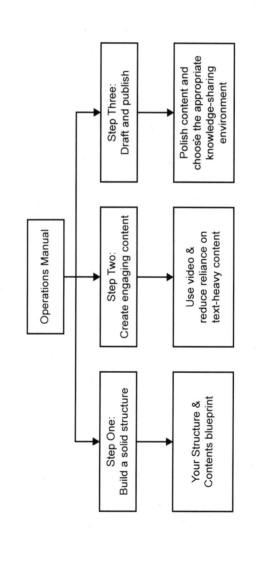

Operations Manual

Step One:
Build a solid structure

Step Two:
Create engaging content

Step Three:
Draft and publish

Your Structure &
Contents blueprint

Use video &
reduce reliance on
text-heavy content

Polish content and
choose the appropriate
knowledge-sharing
environment

1
Understanding The Basics

Imagine franchising as an exquisite culinary journey, with business format franchising representing
a renowned chef's secret recipe. This recipe encom-
passes a meticulously curated list of ingredients;
the franchisor's name, products, services, Business
System, and precise instructions that guide the preparation of a delectable dish – the franchisor's established
business model.

The franchisor (the master chef) reaps the rewards
of sharing their recipe through increased recognition and royalties, while the franchisee (the eager
apprentice) benefits from a tried-and-true recipe that
guarantees a mouthwatering result, pleasing the pal-
ates of their customers.

In this scenario, the Operations Manual is the indispensable cookbook, offering franchisees a clear, step-by-step roadmap to replicate the franchisor's signature dish flawlessly. Without this trusty guide, franchisees would struggle to maintain the same level of quality and consistency, ultimately disappointing their customers' discerning tastebuds. Just as a comprehensive cookbook is essential for a cook's successful replication of a culinary masterpiece, a well-crafted Operations Manual is vital for a franchisee's triumph in implementing the franchisor's proven Business System.

By the end of this chapter, you will:

- Learn the key provisions of the franchise agreement relating to the Operations Manual.

- Understand why you need a manual – and what could happen if you don't provide your franchisees with access to a copy.

- Understand the essence of quality, consistency and conformity.

- Use your smartphone camera to capture the *Manual Magic* Library QR code, where you will find additional tools and resources to help you develop your Operations Manual.

Basics of business format franchising

Franchising is a business model that has become increasingly popular in the modern business world. Business format franchising is one of the main types of franchising. This type of franchising involves the franchisor giving the franchisee rights to use the franchisor's name, products, services and Business System.

Business format franchising is a proven business model that benefits both the franchisor and the franchisee. The franchisor benefits from expanding its business and increasing revenue, while the franchisee benefits from the franchisor's established Business System and brand recognition.

Types of business format franchises

There are four types of business format franchises to consider:

- **Single-unit franchise:** The single-unit franchise is the most common type of franchise. It's a franchise model where the franchisee operates a single location. The franchisee receives the right to use the franchisor's name, products, services and Business System. The franchisee pays the franchisor an initial fee and ongoing fees – eg, service and marketing.

- **Multi-unit franchise:** The multi-unit franchise is a franchise where the franchisee operates multiple locations.

- **Area developer franchise:** The area developer franchise is a franchise where the franchisee has the right to develop and operate a specific geographical area. The area developer franchisee can establish their locations or sub-franchise to other franchisees within the designated area. The area developer franchisee pays an initial fee and ongoing fees – eg, service and marketing.

- **Master franchise:** The master franchise is where the franchisee has the right to develop and sub-franchise a specific geographical area. The master franchisee has the right to develop the franchise system and the recruitment and training of franchisees. The master franchisee pays an initial fee and ongoing fees – eg, service and marketing.

Characteristics of business format franchises

- A well-defined Business System and concept.

- Brand recognition and reputation.

- Ongoing support, training and guidance from franchisors.

- Protection of intellectual property rights.

- Standardised products and services.

- Marketing and advertising support from franchisors.

Examples

The franchises listed below are the traditional business format franchise categories. However, with the growing diversity of franchise systems, the lines are becoming blurred. One example is the large and fast-growing genre of children's activities and entertainment:

- **Retail franchises:** Retail franchises operate in brick-and-mortar stores or shops. Examples include clothing stores, supermarkets and speciality stores. Retail franchises typically require a larger investment due to the costs associated with renting or buying a physical location and stocking inventory.

- **Service franchises:** Service franchises provide customers with a wide range of services such as cleaning, repairs or maintenance. These franchises may operate from a physical location or be mobile, depending on the nature of the service.

- **Van-based franchises:** Van-based franchises are mobile businesses that operate from a vehicle like a van or truck. Van-based franchises often provide home maintenance, cleaning or food delivery services. This type of franchise typically requires a lower initial investment, as franchisees need only invest in the vehicle and necessary equipment.

It's difficult to make the distinction between service and van-based franchises since many service franchises operate via one or more vans.

- **Home-based franchises:** Home-based franchises operate from the franchisee's home, offering flexibility and lower overhead costs. Home-based franchises can include businesses like consulting, online retail or tutoring services such as the AA and BSM Driving Schools.

- **Business-to-business (B2B) franchises:** Business-to-business (B2B) franchises focus on providing products or services to other businesses. Examples include office supplies, commercial cleaning and printing services.

- **Restaurants and food franchises:** Restaurants and food franchises operate in the food industry, including quick-service restaurants (QSRs), fast-casual dining, full-service restaurants, cafés (eg, Costa Coffee) and specialised food concepts.

- **Health and fitness franchises:** Health and fitness franchises focus on the wellness industry, offering services such as gyms, yoga studios and weight loss centres.

- **Educational franchises:** Educational franchises provide learning and enrichment opportunities such as tutoring, test preparation and childcare services. However, children's activity and entertainment franchises such as Razzamataz, Stagecoach Performing Arts, Tappy Toes, Tumble Tots and The Creation Station are educational, while being more about entertainment and enrichment.

- **Personal care franchises:** Personal care franchises cater to personal grooming and wellness needs, including hair salons, spas and massage therapy centres.

- **Automotive franchises:** Automotive franchises provide vehicle maintenance and repair services such as dent and paintwork repair, tyre sales and car washes.

Why do I need an Operations Manual?

After the franchise agreement has been signed, the Operations Manual ('The Manual') is the essential tool in the franchisee's box to set up the new franchise and run the business daily. A comprehensive, practical, up-to-date manual is at the heart of every successful franchise. It's a comprehensive guide for the franchisee/manager and their team on how to:

- Conduct business ethically.

- Create a secure, profitable and lasting business.

- Protect the franchisor's system and the franchisee's investment.

- Maintain quality standards and consistency of products and services.

- Guarantee that the brand is presented professionally and consistently.

- Work together more efficiently and effectively – ie, franchisees can potentially do less and accomplish more.

- Implement an ongoing monitoring system to ensure quality management and compliance.

- Avoid recruiting team members who do not share the same traits and values as the franchisor.

- Troubleshoot problems and find solutions.

- Resolve any disputes between the franchisor and franchisee, such as breach of the agreement.

- Renew the franchise term or sell the business.

Further, the process of documenting the franchisor's know-how and the Business System allows you to:

- Hone and sharpen the business model through continuous improvement.

- Be precise with who is a good fit (or not) for the business, and how best to engage with them.

- Emphasise the value of the franchise offered to your franchisees.

In addition to being a contractual requirement, a comprehensive, well-designed Operations Manual is an asset that helps you to:

- Protect your IP. When trade secrets are written down, they're protected by copyright.

- Ensure that the brand is presented professionally and consistently.

- Implement an ongoing monitoring system to assure quality management and compliance.

Some franchisees argue that the Operations Manual is written merely to protect the franchisor, but this isn't true of any ethical franchisor with whom I have worked to create a new manual, upgrade it or convert a traditional procedures manual to a franchise model.

What if I don't have a manual?

Because it is a contractual obligation, technically, you will breach a fundamental obligation of the franchise agreement when your first franchisee signs up. You also won't be able to reflect any changes, modifications or techniques to the content, because there's no manual to update – another contractual obligation.

Importantly, your know-how and the Business System will be unprotected, so anyone working in the business could steal your ideas to start a similar business. Without an Operations Manual, it can be challenging and expensive to prove someone is 'passing off' your franchise concept as their own.

Yes, it happens! Some years ago, I was approached by a franchisor who had launched a car valeting franchise. He asked if I could help him with his Operations Manual. Having been a former franchisee of a well-known car valeting franchise, he was excited to be launching his new franchise. There was nothing particularly unusual about it; franchisees do leave to launch their own businesses. However, very few would risk asking a British Franchise Association accredited professional advisor to find all mentions of their previous franchisor in the Operations Manual and simply replace them with the name of their new franchise!

David Costello, Head of Franchising, NatWest Bank plc (1999-2001), says,

> 'Having been a banker specialising in franchising, and later a franchise development consultant helping businesses adopt the

franchise model as their chosen method of expansion, I have seen a wide variation in the quality of Operations Manuals issued by franchisors to their franchisees.

'A good quality manual will be intelligently structured, professionally drafted and edited. This enables a franchisee to access information quickly and follow the necessary steps to ensure compliance with the franchisor's proven Business System. Carefully following the methods and procedures described in the manual will give the franchisee the best opportunity of establishing competitive advantage to achieve optimum performance and results.

'Conversely, poorly written examples that are repetitive, ambiguous, or comprising little more than a collection of supposedly motivational statements, are barely worth the paper they are printed on. Generally, a poor Operations Manual reflects a flawed franchise system.'

As a quasi-legal document, the Operations Manual must underpin the franchise agreement and the obligations with which all franchisees must comply, and it must be balanced by documenting those obligations with which the franchisor must comply.

Central to these obligations is confirmation in the manual that you will fully support your franchisees with advice and guidance. You want them to succeed and become profitable and they must feel supported. Many franchisees have little or no previous business management or franchise-specific skills before training and they rely on their franchisor to help them establish a successful business.

Underpinning the franchise agreement

The franchise agreement should contain all the franchisor's and the franchisee's legal rights and obligations, but underpinning those rights and obligations with a well-structured and comprehensive Operations Manual is vital. The franchise agreement and the Operations Manual must complement each other. They must dovetail and be considered together, not in isolation. The manual should be reviewed at least annually. Nina Moran-Watson, British Franchise Association Affiliate Solicitor, says:

'From a legal standpoint, the essence of franchising is licensing the franchisor's intellectual property. Much of that comprises the know-how required to allow replication of the established and successful business format developed by the franchisor. The franchise agreement protects this intellectual property legally, but the Operations Manual sets out the detail of how it must be used.

'Most franchise agreements clearly state that the terms of the Operations Manual are legally binding, but that in the event of any conflict, the terms of the franchise agreement will take precedence. This is important, since it is the breach of the franchise agreement's terms and conditions which would be the basis for any lawful termination of the franchise agreement and/or any claim for damages for breach of contract.

'For that reason, the franchise agreement should be drafted by a specialist franchise solicitor, and no changes should be made to the legal documentation otherwise than through that solicitor. Conversely, one of the great benefits of the Operations Manual is its flexibility. Unlike the franchise agreement, which cannot be varied without the formal consent of both parties, the Operations Manual can be amended from time to time by the franchisor without the consent of, or consultation with, the franchisee. This is extremely useful since it allows the franchisor to reflect changes in operational requirements through the Operations Manual through updates. The business model can be updated and refreshed whenever the franchisor sees fit.

'The Operations Manual should be considered the encyclopaedia of your franchise, detailing every aspect of how to run the business.

It should not itself contain fundamental legal rights and obligations – and certainly not terms and conditions upon which the franchisor is relying to protect its intellectual property and which it may wish to claim breach and terminate the franchise agreement and/or issue proceedings and claim for damages. That is the role of the franchise agreement. Still, failure to comply with the provisions of the Operations Manual can be used as evidence of a breach of the franchise agreement.'

Key provisions relating to the manual[1]

These are the key provisions in the franchise agreement relating to the Operations Manual:

1. **Often contained in the 'Background' or 'Recitals' to the franchise agreement:**

   - 'The Franchisee accepts that it is essential that he complies fully with this Agreement and the Operations Manual.'

   - 'The Franchisee agrees that it is critical to his success and the success of the franchise network that the system is as flexible as possible so that it can respond to commercial

---

1   Key provisions relating to the manual were provided by Nina Moran-Watson, British Franchise Association Affiliate Solicitor.

opportunities and challenges. The Franchisee therefore accepts that the Operations Manual and the system may be changed by the Franchisor from time to time.'

2. **Definition:**

   - '"Operations Manual" means the policies, procedures, methods, processes, techniques and guidance devised and compiled by the Franchisor to be observed and implemented by the Franchisee in operating the Franchisee's business, as amended from time to time, which may be stored electronically by the Franchisor and provided to the Franchisee in hard copy or electronic form or accessed via the internet at the Franchisor's discretion.'

3. **Key clauses:**

   - **Provision:** 'On the successful completion of the initial training, the Franchisor shall make available to the Franchisee the Operations Manual (and any other training materials deemed appropriate by the Franchisor) for the Franchisee's use.'

   - **Adherence:** 'The Franchisee shall operate the Franchisee's business strictly in accordance with the provisions of the Operations Manual and to conform in all respects and at all times with the system as modified from time to time.'

'The Franchisee must conduct the Franchisee's business strictly in accordance with the Operations Manual, the terms of which shall be deemed incorporated into and shall form part of the agreement. In the event of any conflict between the terms of the agreement and the terms of the Operations Manual the terms of the agreement shall prevail.'

- **Updates:** 'Throughout the term of the agreement, the Franchisor will provide the Franchisee with details of any alterations or variations to the Operations Manual, at its discretion, in writing, in electronic form and/or accessed via the internet, to enable the Franchisee to keep the copy in his possession up to date.'

However: 'The Franchisor will ensure that any changes to the Operations Manual will not fundamentally alter the business without prior discussion with the Franchisee.' (Obligation of good faith.)

- **Ownership:** 'The Operations Manual shall at all times remain the Franchisor's sole and exclusive property and the Franchisee acknowledges that the copyright in the Operations Manual vests in the Franchisor (or third parties identified in the Operations Manual) and the Franchisee will not take and will procure that no other person will take any copies of the Operations Manual without the Franchisor's prior written consent.'

- **Entire agreement:** 'The agreement and the Operations Manual constitute the entire agreement between the parties and supersedes all prior agreements in connection with the subject matter hereof...'

- **Confidentiality/termination:** There will often be a provision within the termination clause enabling the Franchisor to terminate the agreement if the Franchisee discloses (or permits the disclosure of) any part of the Operations Manual or other confidential information. On termination, the Operations Manual and any copies should be returned to the Franchisor.

4. **General notes:** The Operations Manual will also be referenced in respect of specific details (either in definitions or clauses). For example:

- A definition of 'Software' may set out specific software to be used by the franchisee in his business, or it may refer to the Operations Manual so that the franchisor can change the software provider or introduce new software without the need to update/amend the agreement.

- A definition of 'Nominated Supplier' will usually include reference to a list of suppliers (for certain goods and/or services) approved by the franchisor set out in the Operations Manual.

- The Franchisee will be obliged to obtain (and maintain) the insurance specified in the Operations Manual before the start date and to comply with the provisions of the manual in respect of a bank account and payment procedures and the sale of the franchisee's business.

- The Franchisee may be required to comply with policies (eg, social media and internet use policy, staff training requirements, customer complaints policy, anti-bribery policy, etc) in the Operations Manual. Inserting these policies into the manual will enable the franchisor to update such policies as necessary throughout the life of a franchise agreement.

- There will sometimes be criteria in the Operations Manual to cover venue/premises requirements, the vehicle specification and fitout, equipment criteria, etc.

Replicating a successful system

If you don't have a well-designed, easy-to-navigate Operations Manual with clearly-written procedures, how will your franchisees take full advantage of your know-how and faithfully replicate your Business System? They can't. They will be left to interpret your content, which may be very different from what you intended. Suzie McCafferty QFP, Founder and CEO of Platinum Wave Franchising, comments:

> 'Cheap, generic copy-and-pasted manuals do so much damage to the franchise industry. The appeal is obvious – get it done fast and save yourself some money. However, it's a recipe for disaster in the long term.
>
> 'Franchising is about replicating a successful business based on the franchisor's know-how and Business System. Give a franchisee a substandard Operations Manual, and you'll end up with their "best guess" of what the business should be, not a replication of yours (and not what they are paying the franchisor for as part of their franchise package).'

Almost certainly, your system will not be applied uniformly across the network – which is the basic concept of a successful franchise. Franchisees are likely to be off-brand, leading to confusion among customers if different messages, logos and non-standard colours are used in marketing and promotion. The repercussions can be catastrophic. Say, for example, that a franchisee fails to operate according to the laws and regulations covering all food businesses. These laws and regulations protect consumers in many parts of the world, because the food and beverage industry is considered to pose a potential danger to consumers. In this instance, our franchisee operates purely on instinct and what they *think* they know from cooking at home.

Consequently, a young girl with a nut allergy dies after eating a cheese and pickle sandwich made with walnut bread – although this type of bread is not on the franchisor's approved list of products that franchisees are allowed to source. The franchisor has provided training and there is a section in the manual about preparation, labelling and sale of items with nuts. The local health authorities close the franchise and the franchisee/manager is jailed for two years. This is reported in the local, regional and then national press, resulting in permanent damage to the brand.

Customers must be 100% confident that the outlet prepares and serves excellent safe food the first time, every time, in a hygienic and risk-free environment. Therefore, the franchisor should have operated and fully documented a comprehensive food safety management system across the whole food supply chain – from growers or manufacturers through distribution and preparation – to the customer's plate.

Know-how

Know-how is defined as confidentially or closely-held information. This will include technical data, formulas, standards, technical information, specifications, processes, methods, handbooks, raw materials – ie, all information, knowledge, assistance, trade practices and secrets and improvements.

An established franchisor's know-how will have been accumulated over many years – much of it learned the hard way. Know-how will likely be scattered like confetti in files across a digital network. Even in a mature franchise, much good content may be found as hard copy or, most likely, reside in a team member's head. Know-how may live purely in the founder's head in a newly established franchise. Teasing it out to create comprehensive content is key to replicating a process faithfully.

Business system

The Business System is how the franchisee will meet customer expectations by systematically analysing, measuring, comparing and testing all the possibilities of what the customer does or doesn't want. A robust Business System, capable of surviving the highs and lows of a business cycle, is at the heart of any high-performing franchise model and should provide the franchisee with a process to fix their operations – eg, by performing internal and external audits.

A sound Business System will help the franchisor and franchisee reduce costs and prevent the erosion of profits. Applying it to safety, hygiene, quality or getting the job done promptly will give them practical, efficient and repeatable results. It should also provide a clear plan to develop the business and improve top-line performance.

A sound recruitment system, for example, will aim to retain team members for longer and provide suitable training and techniques that enable them to complete their work more efficiently and effectively. Procedures should allow the franchise to integrate new team members swiftly and make it easy for them to understand their roles within the franchise. Being able to suggest new ideas to improve the business is critical. Franchisees should seek to harness their team members' views and creativity and, in the process, increase their engagement.

How the complete Business System works should be rigorously tested and improved. Mistakes will have been made – and corrected – so that the franchisee can benefit from their first day to their last.

Standard Operating Procedures

The franchisor's know-how and Business System will be presented in the Operations Manual as a stand-alone, structured set of Standard Operating Procedures – commonly known as SOPs. SOPs capture organisational knowledge for all repeatable core processes. The franchisor's objective is to ensure that the franchisee gets a reliable result the first time, every time. To quote Aristotle: 'We are what we repeatedly do. Excellence, then, is not an act but a habit.'[2]

In a franchise, SOPs are detailed instructions describing how to execute routine activities or tasks. They're designed to ensure that every step in a process is explicitly defined, leading to consistency and uniformity of performance and reducing miscommunication. Compliance with SOPs is essential for achieving standards and operational excellence, as they describe the 'ideal' way a process should be performed, and lead to:

- **Efficiency:** SOPs lay out the best way to perform a task or process, eliminating waste, reducing errors and saving time. When franchise team members follow SOPs, they increase the efficiency of operations.

- **Consistency:** By standardising procedures, SOPs ensure consistency in performance and output. This uniformity enhances product and service quality, a critical component of operational excellence.

- **Compliance:** In addition to the franchise agreement, most franchises operate to regulatory standards that must be met. SOPs that are designed with these regulations in mind ensure compliance, reducing the risk of fines, sanctions and reputation damage.

---

2   Aristotle, *Nicomachean Ethics*

Operational audits

Operational audits are systematic reviews of effectiveness, efficiency and adherence to policies, regulations and procedures within an organisation. An operational audit evaluates the SOPs in action, measuring whether they're being followed and if they're having the desired effect. The goal is to identify operational improvements and increase efficiency. Operational audits often identify areas for improvement in the SOPs. This continuous loop of evaluation and improvement drives operational excellence by constantly refining processes and procedures to optimise results.

Link between SOPs and operational audits

SOPs and operational audits are fundamental components of the business operational framework, with a significant impact on quality control, compliance and operational excellence.

The primary role of operational audits is to review and assess whether SOPs are being followed correctly and effectively, and whether they're contributing to the overall goals and objectives of the organisation. An audit reviews the activities performed, the way they're performed, and the results, and then compares them with what's described in the SOPs. This comparison enables them to find discrepancies, areas of non-compliance and inefficiencies.

There's a growing expectation for franchisors to support their franchisees by providing, interpreting and benchmarking financial information and data. Franchisors have a vested interest in their franchisees being financially successful. If the franchisee is unprofitable, runs out of cash and goes bust, the franchisor loses the income from management service fees or royalties. David Costello, former Head of Franchising at NatWest Bank Plc (1999-2001) and Franchise Consultant, explains:

> 'A prudent franchisor will develop a system, set out in the Operations Manual, to obtain critical financial data from their franchisees – eg, sales revenue, margins, areas of expenditure such as salaries, etc – and then feed the information back to them, and maybe the rest of the network, so that all franchisees can see how each is performing against other similar businesses.

> 'Financial data is just one way of assessing how a business is performing. In 1992, The Harvard Business Review published an article, "The Balanced Scorecard – Measures That Drive Performance", authored by accounting academic Dr Robert Kaplan and business theorist Dr David Norton.[3] Their work took previous performance measures

---

3   RS Kaplan and DP Norton, 'The balanced scorecard – measures that drive performance', *HBR* (Jan-Feb 1992), https://hbr.org/1992/01/the-balanced-scorecard-measures-that-drive-performance-2, accessed 3 July 2023

and adapted them to include non-financial information. Corporates across the globe have since adopted the concept of measuring and improving their performance across a range of measurable parameters called Key Performance Indicators, often termed KPIs.

'The Balanced Scorecard model typically involves collecting and analysing information from four aspects of a business: Financial, Customer, Learning & Growth *and* Organisational Development. How the final two are expressed varies, but Financial and Customer are constant across most companies and sectors. SMART targets are set for several measurables, or KPIs, in each area. SMART means Specific, Measurable, Achievable, Relevant and Time-based. The idea is to produce a scorecard showing how each business unit, or franchisee, is performing relative to targets and their peers.

'Well-organised franchise networks could use The Balanced Scorecard model as a performance monitoring and motivational tool. The results may also form part of a rewards and incentives programme with awards for their top franchisees in each category.

'Typically, Financial measurables – KPIs or targets – are aspects such as sales, costs/expenditure, margins, etc. For customers, perspectives are collected to gauge customer satisfaction, such as customer surveys, wait times or other forms of objective feedback. At one of my former employers, the third category was changed to "Internal Quality" and measured using Mystery Shopper scores. At another former employer, the Learning & Growth KPI was how up-to-date the office was with completing a range of mandatory internal training courses.

'There are many benefits to using The Balanced Scorecard approach, the most critical being to distil information from across a variety of areas into a single report. This can save time, money and resources when assessing performance and comparing franchisees – perhaps even against company-owned outlets – and quickly identify where improvement is required.'

Adherence to SOPs and their evaluation through operational audits form a cycle of continuous improvement, fostering operational excellence. This relationship is an important part of achieving and maintaining high standards of quality, efficiency and compliance in a franchise.

Quality

Quality is everything that adds up to providing complete customer satisfaction so that the franchisee can build on the franchisor's desire to be the customer's

'No.1 Choice' – eg, extensive choice of locations, highly trained personnel, longer opening hours. It is superior in knowledge, selling skills and all-around professionalism and essential in communicating the franchisor's vision and brand values – it's their DNA. This will lead to more loyal customers who become great brand advocates and, ultimately, 'Raving Fans for Life'.[4] A phrase coined by Ken Blanchard and Sheldon Bowles in their book *Raving Fans: A Revolutionary Approach to Customer Service*, a 'Raving Fan for Life' is more loyal, spends more, and refers more unsolicited leads.

Perception of quality

Quality is critical, no matter where we are and what the product or service may be. Quality is in the eye of the beholder. Our perception of quality can also change many times during a lifetime. Remember the thin, synthetic shirt made with nylon or polyester – the shirt that crackled with static when you took it off? It was easy to wash, drip-dry, non-iron, practical, cheap – and uncomfortable to wear, especially in hot weather. It suited a lifestyle and a budget. Next came the more expensive cotton shirt that was gentle on the skin, comfortable and kept us fresh longer, whatever the season. Finally, the elegance and sophistication

---

4   K Blanchard and S Bowles, *Raving Fans: A Revolutionary Approach to Customer Service* (Harper, 1 September 2011)

of a silk shirt moulding softly to the body, conveying a pleasant sensation of freshness, smoothness and softness to the touch – the epitome, to some, of exceptional quality.

Whatever their personal perception of quality, the franchise team must understand that franchise quality must conform to the customer's needs and expectations. It's the franchisor's task to communicate their and their customer's perception of 'quality' through the Operations Manual. Descriptions such as 'best, highest, exceptional' and 'good' are inadequate. They don't convey anything to the reader, so this description must be qualified to avoid any confusion.

Summary

- Providing your franchisees with a copy of your Operations Manual on signing the franchise agreement and keeping it up to date are fundamental obligations.

- Transferring know-how and faithfully replicating the Business System helps franchisees succeed and become profitable.

- Standard Operating Procedures (SOPs) and Operational Audits are fundamental components of the business operational framework, with a significant impact on quality control, compliance and operational excellence.

- Whatever their personal perception of quality, the franchise team must understand that franchise quality must conform to the customer's needs and expectations.

2
Planning Your Project

Taking sufficient time to consider the many elements that must come together for an Operations
Manual is like the careful planning and preparation
that goes into baking a cake. Each ingredient, or element of the manual, needs to be properly measured
and prepared for the recipe – the Operations Manual –
to work.

Knowing who to take on your journey is like choosing the right tools and assistants for your baking
process. Just as you wouldn't try to mix a cake batter with a whisk unfit for purpose, you need the right
team members and resources to create an effective
Operations Manual.

In April 1979, a decade into my career as a journalist, I was covering socio-economic issues in the Arabian Gulf. A group of ex-pats had just finished playing table tennis in the basement of the Gulf Hotel, Muscat. Knowing journalists have a taste for adventure, a blonde, blue-eyed German ex-pat ending his tour of duty with Oman TV directed his question at me: 'I don't suppose anyone would keep me company when I drive my car home to Stuttgart?' This wasn't just a trip in a rare sports car with a good-looking guy. It was an expedition across fourteen countries. To be more precise – three thousand miles and much of it desert; some of it hostile. We'd need a Carnet de Passage and multiple visas, including one for the Kingdom of Saudi Arabia. Saudi visas for women are like hen's teeth, but successful navigation of the disintegrating Saudi pipeline route depended on us reaching the Syrian port of Latakia and catching the ferry to Brindisi. Cutting out Turkey was vital because of political violence and the death squads.

Undaunted, and thanks to my Omani sponsors, their connections, and multiple strings pulled in the background, our challenge became a reality. Seventy-two hours later, Jürgen and I had our visas, our route mapped with timelines, and our accommodation booked to get us home 21 days from setting off. We travelled light with necessities, but had everything we needed in case of emergencies for the journey – plus a contingency plan. This was just as well. The only ferry for a week from Latakia had left the day before, leaving us no alternative but to drive through Eastern Turkey.

An unforeseen fuel crisis and curfews in Ankara and Istanbul almost led to abandoning the car and flying home. But we made it on time, and on budget!

By the end of this chapter, you will:

- Know when to appoint a Project Coordinator and their role.

- Understand who (apart from you) must be involved.

- Learn why conducting a survey with your franchisees is essential.

- Use your smartphone camera to capture the *Manual Magic* Library QR code to access an example Franchisee Questionnaire with a covering email.

Project planning

Creating an Operations Manual, like the adventurous cross-country journey described earlier, requires meticulous planning, attention to detail and adaptability.

Initially, it's about gathering the 'ingredients' or information – the guidelines, procedures and best practices that make your franchise unique. This is akin to obtaining the necessary visas for the journey. Not having the right information can impede progress, just as not having the right visas did.

The journey's route is comparable to the manual's structure. You must plan out your route – or structure – carefully, deciding which sections to include and in what order they should appear. This will help your franchisees navigate the manual effectively, much like a well-planned route aided the travellers.

Just as I relied on my Omani sponsors and connections, creating an Operations Manual isn't a solitary task. It requires input from various stakeholders, including franchisees, managers and other team members whose expertise and experience enhance the manual's effectiveness.

Finally, just as I successfully reached Germany, a well-planned, thoughtfully created Operations Manual will guide your franchisees towards success. It reflects your journey as a franchisor, filled with learned lessons and best practices, forming a roadmap for others to follow. And, like the journey, it's a dynamic document that will require changes and adaptations as the franchise evolves, continuing the journey towards success.

Appointing a Project Coordinator

The Project Coordinator manages the complete three-step process from concept to publication. If you hold all the franchise know-how, that's you! If you can get a team of company experts together, small or large, you will likely be the Project Coordinator – or you can appoint one.

The Project Coordinator needs good organisational skills and must be methodical and proactive. They must be capable of guiding their team of experts through each step of the process so that all content is approved for publication and published on time and within budget.

Role of the Project Coordinator

The Project Coordinator plays a crucial role like a master baker. They bring together team members and franchisees to ensure that all the necessary elements come together at the right time for a perfect result. The Project Coordinator should act as a facilitator or 'conduit' for information between the various team members.

As the Project Coordinator, it's important to ensure the smooth running of the project. This involves keeping track of the project's progress, maintaining communication with all team members and effectively delegating tasks. The Project Coordinator should be a central point of contact for any questions or concerns during the project's lifecycle. You will read more about this in Chapter 4, Drawing Up Your Project Plan. The Project Coordinator should:

- Establish a transparent chain of command.

- Obtain buy-in from everyone involved.

- Build a strong rapport with team members.

- Set goals and expectations early.

- Be an active listener.

They must also be able to strike a balance between pressing team members too hard and coaching them gently to meet content delivery, production, and publication dates. Critically, the Project Coordinator, as owner or franchise operations director, is responsible for signing off each element of the Operations Manual ready for publication.

Understanding the challenges

Comments Jo Middleton:

'The manual breaks down the proven business model so the franchisee can implement the processes and build the franchise from a start-up into a successful, profitable business if they follow the franchisor's Standard Operating Procedures. All the franchisor's know-how should be crammed into the manual, including the real nitty-gritty of running the franchise daily. This will include bookkeeping and accountancy procedures and protocols for dealing with customer complaints through renewal procedures and strategies for exiting the business.

'Franchisees and their teams must faithfully replicate the successful business model. Content should be geared to the different individual learning styles. This means making the manual's content easily accessible, clear, stimulating and, therefore, more engaging using mixed media such as text, video, audio, images, real-world examples, graphs, etc.'

Teamwork

Team members have different ideas, opinions and working styles. Getting them all on board can be challenging. You will need to understand everyone's strengths, weaknesses and motivations so that you can utilise their skills and make them feel valued. When dealing with an entire team, you should include everyone in the decision-making process so they feel that their voices are heard and their contributions are appreciated. Encourage teamwork and collaboration among your team members, and be supportive if integrating their work on the Operations Manual with their day jobs creates any additional pressure.

Teamwork is essential for success, so encourage your team members and franchisees to work together whenever possible instead of independently – unless there's a good reason not to. For example, if two people have expertise in marketing and promotion, they should collaborate.

Having clear communication channels

Ensure everyone understands what they need to do, why they need to do it and when they need to complete it. You may need to repeat yourself a few times to make sure that everyone understands each step of the process. This means they must be aware of everything happening daily so they can respond quickly if anything needs addressing urgently:

- **Be consistent with your expectations:** Everyone must understand what is expected of them from day one so there are no surprises and everyone works to the same plan.

- **Be patient:** Encourage people struggling or going off track by making suggestions and offering advice as appropriate.

- **Set deadlines:** Strict deadlines help keep projects on track, so set them upfront so people know what needs to be done and by when. This is particularly important when several people, who don't work at one location or on similar schedules, are involved in the project, which was the case when we developed the Costa Coffee Operational Manual. Costa's project coordinator was based in Dubai and functional heads were located in the UK, as was I.

Team engagement

It's crucial to explain to your team the importance of providing franchisees with a new or upgraded Operations Manual, as it serves as the foundation of a franchise. Your team should understand how this manual differs from other business models and the significance of uniformity, conformity and delivering to your customers' perception of quality products/services. This will lead to satisfied customers who will return and spread the word. It's essential to stress that a comprehensive, well-structured Operations Manual is a key differentiator. All stakeholders need to understand that:

- It's a legal requirement for franchised (and many licensed) businesses.

- It plays a vital role in the success of the franchised business.

- This is not just an operational document – it's strategic and commercial.

- The manual is built around the Balanced Scorecard Model[5] and Total Quality Management (TQM).

---

5 The Balanced Scorecard is a management system that enables organisations to translate the vision and strategy into action. It provides feedback on internal business processes and external outcomes to continually improve organisational performance and results. Robert Kaplan and David Norton created the balanced scorecard approach in the early 1990s. See also https://balancedscorecard.org/bsc-basics-overview.

They must also be made aware of:

- The likely scope of the work involved.

- The start date and the ideal time for publication.

- Who will be involved – eg, the franchisee network or a formally appointed franchisee panel, IT support and, perhaps, a designer.

If you decide to make your manual visually appealing, you will need to involve your in-house design team or an independent designer from the outset.

Kwik-Fit used an external designer for their online manual and chose to print limited prestige editions for newly appointed Master Franchisees. The AA's in-house team designed content for the Learning Management System, but initially printed beautifully designed copies of the AA & BSM Driving School Manual for management and driving instructors.

Before the advent of online editions, Costa Coffee's suite of volumes for their Operational Manual was packaged in an attractive presentation box. Subsequently, individual volumes were issued on CD-ROM.

Consultation period

Depending on the size of the business and your team, you should consider setting up one or multiple awareness workshops before you start working on the structure of your Operations Manual. You should set up workshops with your:

- Content owners – ie, the franchisor's experts who will contribute the content.

- Pilot franchisees prior to launch.

- A franchisee panel, appointed if you're a mature franchise.

You should make them aware that you are developing a new Operations Manual or upgrading one that's out of date. This is an excellent opportunity to obtain feedback from those with expert knowledge and practical experience within the business.

If you are piloting one or more franchises, or have a mature network, don't miss this golden opportunity to involve your franchisee(s) in the awareness and consultation process. The aim is to:

- Communicate why you're creating or upgrading your Operations Manual and its value to the network going forwards.

- Obtain their views about what information needs to be included in your Operations Manual for current and future franchisees.

- Ensure everyone is on board with the project's scope and role.

Timing

The Operations Manual must be available for the launch of the new franchise. On upgrading, publication could coincide with the annual franchise conference or another important event in your franchise calendar.

Timing is always a tricky issue. Most clients believe they will have their manual ready in a couple of months. Reality is different because, depending on whether they are new or mature, they either underestimate the magnitude of the IP they hold in their databases and what must be created, or the lack of documented IP and the magnitude of what must be created.

For Costa Coffee Brand Partners, we developed the 2006/8 version of the Core Operating Brand Standards volume first for the Costa System Operational Manual. However, because of the size of the franchise, we subsequently created separate volumes to cover New Business Setup & Support, Food & Beverage, Marketing, Property, Supply Chain, Health, Safety & Hygiene and People.

Engaging franchisees

When setting up your franchise, it's important to value the opinions of your franchisees, especially in the beginning stages, since the Franchisee/Manager and team members will be founder members using the Operations Manual. It's beneficial to encourage them to continuously provide suggestions on how to improve the manual. This will ensure your manual becomes a 'living document' reflecting continuous improvement.

Regardless of when you plan to upgrade your manual, you should develop a procedure for periodic feedback – including best practice. You should welcome their input to ensure they feel engaged in the process.

Franchisee panel

If you operate a mature franchise, you may well have appointed a franchisee panel involving three or four experienced franchisees. Engaging them in the manual development process as part of your team will ensure you cover what they want instead of the information you think they need.

If you are at the pre-launch stage and don't have enough staff to form an in-house team, you should invite your pilot franchisee(s) to participate.

Pilot franchises

A pilot franchise is the test phase of a franchise's development. It's where you and your team will test your business model to ensure that it's viable and how best to run it. The concept behind the pilot franchise is to:

- Allow the new franchisor to iron out any wrinkles before making big decisions about whether the franchise will fly.

- See what works and what doesn't before committing to a full-scale launch.

- Ensure that all the elements of the franchisee's business are working together in harmony and that they can sustain them long-term.

Because you will obtain valuable feedback on how well the business model will work in practice rather than just in theory, it would be wise to involve your pilot franchisees in developing your Operations Manual.

The first edition of your Operations Manual (known as your Pilot Operations Manual) should be tested before launching your franchise. Then you can work towards the first complete edition.

Conducting a survey

Surveying your franchisee network is a great way to obtain the information you need to plan the content of your Operations Manual and upgrade it annually.

You should allow sufficient time for everyone to complete the survey. I recommend a 10- to 14-day window.

This is enough time to ensure your franchisees have had the opportunity to complete the survey, but not so much time that they forget about it or get distracted by other things. You can also adjust this based on the information you require.

Online surveys

The best way to conduct a survey is online. Online surveys are best suited for a network of more than ten franchisees, but this isn't set in stone. This way, everyone has access and can answer anonymously if they want to provide more detail or add comments.

Plenty of free survey tools are available online; just pick one that works best for your business needs. SurveyMonkey is one of the world's most popular questionnaire tools. It's a tool that makes survey creation, design and data collection easy for beginners. It provides the flexibility to ask different questions, including open comments, interactive sliders and multiple-choice questions. You can also include questions written by team members in your surveys to make them more effective.

Guaranteeing a good response

Invite your franchisees to take part in the survey. Explain that you are creating/upgrading the Operations Manual to greatly enhance the information, support and guidance you provide. You want to make it the 'go-to' knowledge-sharing resource on all aspects of the business from launch to the sale of their business.

To guarantee a good response, you should offer something of value in exchange for each completed survey, for example:

- A gift card as an incentive for completing the survey.

- Entry of respondents' names into a prize draw.

- A prize for the most comprehensive feedback.

This will demonstrate your interest in their opinion and that you value their contribution. It will also help build loyalty in both parties, increase response rates and ensure that your franchisees take the time to carefully complete the questionnaire.

Survey questions and questionnaire

You should seek your franchisees' views on the fundamental parts of the business and its format. You should aim for ten questions per category. Based on the skeleton for almost every manual I've created, a questionnaire was developed for a client with a network of 50+ franchisees. Using SurveyMonkey, the B2B van-based franchisor asked for feedback on the parts of the Operations Manual that could be improved and the subjects that franchisees considered should be included to make the manual more effective.

Summary

- Taking time to plan an Operations Manual is critical for its success.

- For an extensive network with many stakeholders, appointing a Project Coordinator is essential to manage the development process and maintain clear communication channels.

- Engaging franchisees and obtaining their feedback is critical for continuously improving the manual's content and format.

- Encouraging teamwork and collaboration among all team members is essential for success.

- Surveys are an effective way to obtain feedback from franchisees and continuously improve your Operations Manual.

- Offering incentives encourages your franchisees to complete surveys, demonstrates an interest in franchisees' opinions and helps to build loyalty.

3
Building Your Structure & Contents

Creating content without structure is like throwing a bunch of ingredients into a mixing bowl without measuring or following a recipe. With no clear direction or purpose, the result is likely to be a disaster. Without a structure, the manual could end up disjointed, confusing and difficult to use, making it less effective in guiding franchisees and ensuring consistency across all locations.

Developing a clear framework for organising and presenting your know-how for your Business System is the first in the three-step process.

The Structure & Contents detailed here will work well regardless of whether you operate a new, developing or mature franchise. When you transform your Operations Manual into a knowledge-sharing environment you can choose one of three main options according to network development and maturity:

- A Core Operating Brand Standards Manual (COBSM) – underpinned by a comprehensive cloud-based resource library / database.

- A Core Operating Brand Standards Manual underpinned by a comprehensive resource library / database accessed via an intranet / franchisee portal to create a knowledge-sharing centre.

- A Core Operating Brand Standards Manual underpinned by a comprehensive resource library / database held on a dedicated knowledge-sharing platform.

By the end of this chapter, you will:

- Know why you must define your readership.

- Learn how to start categorising your Intellectual Property (IP).

- Understand how to develop your framework into a comprehensive structure.

- Use your smartphone camera to capture the *Manual Magic* Library QR code to access an example Structure & Contents for People (Your Team).

Core purposes

Creating a detailed Structure & Contents is the foundation of *any* Operations Manual. It:

- Provides you with the blueprint of your Business System.

- Helps you develop the Project Plan from start to publication.

- Allows you to identify the experts, other than yourself, who will contribute content if your franchise is sufficiently established to operate a Head Office team.

- Helps you identify whether there are any gaps between the IP you have and the IP you need to add/create.

- Is the basis for evaluating the type of content you need to create.

- Is the basis for evaluating where to use more engaging content such as 'show, don't tell' videos for knowledge sharing.

Your franchisee readership

Patisserie Pénélope franchisee

Our case study, Patisserie Pénélope, is a brick-and-mortar single-unit franchise. Successful franchisees can become multi-unit owners, and there are opportunities to set up and operate franchises overseas.

Let's assume that our franchisees need a strong background in the food and hospitality industry, with a focus on pastry arts. This implies an understanding of various pastry techniques, ingredients and food safety regulations.

Expect franchisees to have a basic understanding of business management principles. This will include financial management (budgeting, cash flow management, profit and loss analysis), human resources (hiring, training and employee retention) and marketing (branding, social media promotion and local advertising).

Acknowledge that franchisees may have varying levels of experience with specific aspects of the Patisserie Pénélope business model, such as the procurement of high-quality ingredients, the design and layout of our boutique-style patisserie or the management of customer relations. In these cases, the Operations Manual should provide support and resources to fill any gaps and ensure consistency across all franchise locations.

Domestic cleaning service franchisee

Here, we can assume that franchisees may have a diverse range of backgrounds and experiences, with varying levels of familiarity with the cleaning industry. Some franchisees may have prior experience in the industry. Others may be new to the sector but have strong business management skills.

Expect franchisees to have basic business management skills. These are financial management (budgeting, invoicing and cash flow management), human resources (hiring, training and employee scheduling) and marketing (online promotion, local advertising and customer relationship management). However, they may require additional support and resources in areas where they lack experience or knowledge.

Recognise that franchisees may need more detailed guidance on specific aspects of the cleaning business, such as specialised cleaning techniques (carpet and upholstery cleaning, deep cleaning and eco-friendly cleaning), equipment maintenance and usage, inventory management and regulatory compliance (health and safety regulations, insurance requirements and waste disposal). The Operations Manual should address these topics to ensure consistent quality and professionalism across all franchise locations.

Master franchisee (regional or country developer)

We can assume that master franchisees have a strong background in business management, leadership and strategic planning. They should have experience in franchise development, regional expansion or similar business growth initiatives, which implies an understanding of market analysis, location selection and franchisee recruitment.

Expect master franchisees to have a solid understanding of the local market conditions, cultural context and regulatory environment in their assigned region or country. This includes knowledge of consumer preferences, competitive landscape, legal requirements (business registration, permits and licences), and any specific challenges or opportunities unique to the region.

Recognise that master franchisees may require additional support and resources in specific areas. This includes international supply chain management (import/export regulations, customs and logistics), cross-cultural communication (language barriers, cultural norms and etiquette) or localised marketing strategies (targeted advertising, partnerships and events). The Operations Manual should provide guidance and resources to help master franchisees navigate these complexities and ensure the successful growth of the franchise network in their territory.

Every franchise is unique, regardless of whether they operate in the same sector. It's your culture – 'how we do things around here' – that creates your identity.

Simple concepts

'My franchise is a simple concept,' I often hear a client say. 'Surely there can't be many procedures to document?' Well, franchisors with simple concepts are often surprised when we take the first step to draw up a comprehensive Structure & Contents for their manual from the franchise agreement and other IP.

Take the Operations Manual we developed for Unigate Dairies at the end of the Nineties, with nearly 2,000 franchisees. Self-employed home delivery salesmen delivered milk and a few groceries to customers on their round and collected money due at the end of the month. What could be simpler! Yet the manual we created ran to two volumes, with a third planned.

The Franchisee Quality Manual covered every routine from establishment of the business, training and running their own business through customer service and health and safety. It comprised 120 pages with fifty appendices.

The Quality Franchise Manual covered the franchise and hire agreements, obligations, administration and financial controls. This ran to eighty pages with thirty appendices.

When you identify all the critical processes for setting up a new franchise and the daily, weekly, monthly, quarterly and annual routines that franchisees and their teams must perform to your quality standards and continuously improve, there's a lot of information to cover. In addition, everything must be measured, analysed and improved via self and annual operational audits. Consider your franchisee's perspective and what will be most helpful and engaging for them. Your Structure & Contents must be organised in a way that makes sense to them and include descriptive titles and headings that accurately reflect the content of each section. (See Chapter 10, Elements Of A Good Draft.)

You will need to create the structure commensurate with the type of franchisee reading your Operations Manual. For example, when we constructed Costa Coffee's original volumes for Brand Partners, we covered information appropriate to a senior executive's skills and responsibilities for developing a region or country. When we communicated with the AA Driving Instructors, we assumed little or no prior management experience.

Research fundamentals

Research involves finding, collecting, organising and analysing the company's IP (ie, information/assets) that you hold digitally in a database (usually spread across folders on your computer) and in printed materials. Whether scattered around the filing system or structured as a formal resource library or knowledge centre, you probably hold more information than you realise. This will provide you with a rich seam of topics for inclusion in the Structure & Contents.

As a new franchisor, your resources may be limited to a final draft of your franchise agreement, business plan and marketing materials. These will provide the foundation for developing a comprehensive Structure & Contents. As a mature franchisor, upgrading your current Operations Manual will be easier, because you can use this to reverse-outline the structure.

You will need to reference these documents to specify systems, processes and procedures relevant to your franchise.

Franchise agreement

The franchise agreement is the key document to help map your Structure & Contents. In simple terms, the franchise agreement is *what* you and your franchisee must do to fulfil your obligations.

The Operations Manual explains the operational details: *how* you and your franchisees must meet these obligations, *why* and *when* your franchisees must meet them and *what else* they must consider in the process.

Legislation and regulation

Other legal and regulatory requirements are likely to affect day-to-day operations. Franchisees must be aware of these laws and regulations and how they directly affect daily operations. Examples include company law, taxation, employment, health and safety, hygiene, environmental, planning, data protection and criminal record checks. You must include any licences your franchisees need to obtain to run their business and the rules, policies and procedures they and your employees must comply with.

Government websites provide up-to-date information. When you come to write about it, you don't need to reproduce it verbatim. An introductory paragraph with a hyperlink to the relevant, current URL is all that's required to point your franchisees to the credible source.

Business plan

Your business plan and your franchisees' business plans provide a wealth of information you can use to develop the structure of your Operations Manual:

- **Executive summary:** This provides valuable information on who you are and what you offer, your mission and vision statements, your objectives (including financial goals and growth strategies) and a description of your target market and how your franchisees will reach it.

- **Business description:** This explains what the franchise does, who it serves and how it serves them. It is usually broken down into multiple parts. It describes the components of your Business System, including your history, products/services, pricing structure, marketing strategy and financial projections at least three years into the future. It should also include information about patents or trademarks relevant to your business.

- **Market analysis:** This includes information about the market for your products.

- **Market strategies:** These explain how to reach customers and grow profits through effective marketing and sales initiatives that align with the business goals and values.

- **Competitor analysis:** This is where competitors' strengths and weaknesses are listed to identify opportunities for differentiation in the marketplace based on their performance over time or absence in certain areas. This includes customer service quality or product variety offered at different price points within a given category like a patisserie, products sold instore and the ordering of special occasion cakes online – eg, Christmas, Easter, Eid, Diwali, birthday and christening.

- **Design and development plan:** This describes how this product or service will look after being designed based on feedback from focus groups conducted during the initial research stages before anything was created.

- **Financial information:** This covers how much it costs to open a new location, the management service fee / royalty / marketing levy charged each month and how much the franchisee will earn from it. However, don't include financial projections that could be construed as a profit forecast or a guarantee.

- **Products or services:** These include competitors' strengths and weaknesses and local demographics such as population growth rate, which may affect sales.

Marketing collateral

Marketing collateral – also known as sales collateral or marketing materials – is any printed, digital or visual material that you create to help build awareness of your brand by creating interest in who you are, what you do and why people should choose to work with your franchisees over someone else. To help you develop your structure, here are some examples of marketing collateral:

- Logo, strapline, brand colours and signage

- Mission, vision, core values and sustainability statements

- Service level agreements

- Website and social media profiles

- Blog posts and podcasts

- eBooks or guides (eg, brand guidelines)

- Newspaper, magazine and social media advertisements (eg, Facebook, LinkedIn and Twitter)

- Advertorials, testimonials and case studies

- Company presentations and 'how-to' videos

- Brochures, leaflets, posters and flyers

- Customer welcome packs

- Original graphics

- Reports and research projects

- Company-branded clothing (eg, workwear and name badges) and branded merchandise (eg, mugs and pens)

If you have a design playbook or similar, this should provide you with all the specifications your franchisees need for site selection, suitable premises, building and fitting out and equipping the new franchise to be on brand. If you have a design playbook, you do not need to reproduce it in full. Simply add a one-paragraph description with a hyperlink.

Employee handbook

An employee handbook sets out franchise policies, procedures and rules by which employees and employers must abide. Breaches are dealt with through the disciplinary process. If you have an employee handbook, you do not need to reproduce it in full. Simply add a one-paragraph description with a hyperlink.

Training materials

Training materials and well-designed content effectively communicate expectations and define processes and procedures from onboarding to professional development. The most common are presentations, checklists, worksheets or workbooks, handouts, exercises and activities, procedures documentation, instructor course outlines, forms and self-assessments. Again, you do not need to reproduce these in full. Simply add a one-paragraph description with a hyperlink.

Structure 'musts'

The Structure & Contents that you create for your Operations Manual must underpin all references to 'The Manual' in your franchise agreement. You must also align the Structure & Contents to your reader and it must accurately reflect your goals, standards and procedures.

Your Structure & Contents must be sufficiently detailed to give you or your team members a clear understanding of what content to write for each area of the business and to give franchisees a clear understanding of what is required of them and how to faithfully replicate processes for each area of the business:

- **Be specific:** The Structure & Contents headings and cross-headings should relate to the information needed. A Structure & Contents that is too broad can be confusing and unhelpful.

- **Be flexible:** A Structure & Contents should be flexible enough to allow for changes and revisions as the franchise evolves. Don't be too rigid. Be open to making changes and adjustments as needed. Comments Luke Frey, CEO, Bella Vista Executive Advisors:

  'Writing an operations manual requires striking a balance between providing clear guidelines and allowing for flexibility, all while distinguishing mandatory practices from recommended best practices. In addition, a system for consistent communication and review between franchisors and franchisees is crucial to ensure the manual remains relevant and practical. With careful consideration, attention to detail, and an open line of communication, an Operations Manual can not only lead to the success of an organisation but also create opportunities for growth and innovation.'

- **Be consistent:** Ensure standard headings are consistent throughout the Structure & Contents. This will help franchisees to follow the flow of the manual more easily.

See also Chapter 7, Underpinning The Franchise Agreement.

Creating a basic framework

To start building a Structure & Contents for your knowledge-sharing environment, you must first create a basic framework. This will help you:

- Focus on the main elements of your Business System

- Identify your assets that connect an audience with your brand

- Organise *all* your IP

It will give you the clarity you need from the chaos that often arises when a business grows organically and when your IP is scattered across digital folders and in physical filing systems.

Main Categories

These are the six main Categories into which your IP should fall. They work well for most types of businesses:

1. **Introduction:** A welcome and introduction to the brand, its history, market, organisation and how to use the manual, key agreements and/or policies, support and contacts, and glossary of company terms.

2. **New Business Setup & Support:** How to get the franchisee's business off to a flying start with a firm foundation to launch and the first year of operation.

3. **People (Your Team):** How to recruit the best team members, train them and motivate them to remain loyal to your business and the brand.

4. **Marketing & Promotion:** How to promote the franchisee's products and services through local marketing and social media.

5. **Day-to-Day Operating Requirements:** How to manage the workplace and help franchisees to achieve a work-life balance.

6. **Development, Growth & Profit:** How to keep your franchisee's finances on track, grow their business, develop new skills, and renew the agreement at the end of the term – or sell the business.

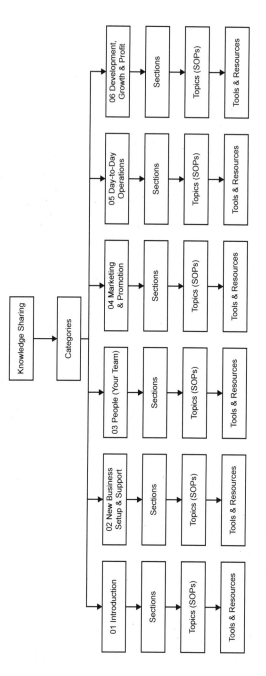

Knowledge-Sharing Structure and Organisation

Creating digital folders

Your first task is to organise all your electronic IP into appropriate Categories until you have identified and named your Sections (ie, each process). The easiest way is to create a digital folder hierarchy for each Category. You will then need to create a sub-folder for each Section, with a companion folder for the Tools & Resources section, into which you will organise relevant IP.

The diagram represents the hierarchy of the six main Categories. Each Category has multiple Sections. Sections must be tailored to your franchise and in a logical order. Each Section breaks down into multiple Topics which represent the SOPs. Each Section is underpinned by relevant Tools & Resources.

Always ensure all folders and files are updated and backed up automatically via a company network or in the cloud. Cloud-based programs such as Dropbox or Microsoft OneDrive can be set up to update automatically.

Creating a hard copy version

You will find it helpful to also build a physical version of your digital manual. Mirror your digital structure by using a separate binder for each Category. Separate the Sections in each binder with dividers and place the Tools & Resources at the back of the Section to which it belongs.

Next, print a screenshot of the Sections under each Category, and of the Tools & Resources for each Section. Place the printouts, as you would a List of Contents, at the front of the relevant Section and its Tools & Resources. Your IP assets are now organised.

Identifying Sections with AI

To add the flesh to your Structure & Contents, start by identifying suitable section titles to each Category. If you find this challenging, ChatGPT and other AI products are versatile tools for identifying and generating Section titles. When prompted correctly, ChatGPT will output suitable Section titles for each Category for evaluation. This saves a great deal of time and can provide an excellent framework for review and, ultimately, content creation.

The secret is to build reliable and high-performing prompts for ChatGPT. This requires an understanding of the key information to be included and the clear and precise framing of questions or statements:

- **Define the context:** Start your prompt with clear context-setting. For instance, if you're asking about suitable Sections for franchise staff recruitment, start with, 'In the context of employee recruitment for a [restaurant chain]...'

- **Be specific:** The more specific you are in your prompts, the more accurate the model's responses will be. For example, instead of, 'What should a franchisee know?' ask, 'What are the key responsibilities of a franchisee in managing people from job descriptions to performance management?'

- **Structure your request:** If you need a detailed response or a structured document, guide the model with the structure you want. For example, for People (Your Team), 'Create a comprehensive list of key Section titles and topics for Human Resources / People Management for a [restaurant] franchise.'

- **Sequence your questions:** For more complex topics, break down your request into multiple questions or statements.

- **Revise as needed:** If the response from the model isn't what you expected, try rephrasing or refining the question to be more explicit about what you need. Remember, developing a franchise Operations Manual is a complex task, so don't hesitate to ask detailed and thorough questions to get the most accurate and comprehensive responses.

Identifying Topics with AI

You will now create the list of Topics that must be covered under each Section. This means you're drilling down to construct a detailed picture of each process.

I've used ChatGPT effectively to develop topics under each Section of a Structure & Contents. AI can provide ideas, guidelines, and recommendations. For example, under Day-to-Day Operating Requirements, say, you need a Section on 'Achieving a Work-Life Balance'.

Here's how you could use ChatGPT to help develop this Section with topics:

Start by providing the context. Mention that you're developing content for a franchise Operations Manual, specifically focusing on the section about achieving a work-life balance for franchisees. For example: 'I am developing content for a franchise Operations Manual and need assistance with the "Achieving a Work-Life Balance" Section. The goal is to provide a list of Topics to help franchisees balance their personal and professional lives effectively.'

Then ask for additional detail. For example: 'Please provide headings and sub-headings of Topics for effective time management strategies for franchisees to balance business operations and personal time.'

Review the content provided by ChatGPT. It may need revision or refinement to fit your specific sector, brand, audience and guidelines. You can also ask follow-up questions or request more detail on any areas that need elaboration.

Reverse-outlining

If you're upgrading your Operations Manual, you can use ChatGPT to create a reverse outline.

To use ChatGPT to reverse-outline your content, you'll need to provide specific examples or brief summaries from the existing manual, and then ask ChatGPT for help in categorising and restructuring them. Here's an example of how you might structure the request:

'Here is a section from my Operations Manual: "All employees must be given proper training on our food handling and safety protocols, including [XYZ] certification. Regular refresher courses should be scheduled every six months." In which of the six Categories (Introduction, New Business Setup & Support, People (Your Team), Marketing & Promotion, Day-to-Day Operating Requirements, Business Development, Growth & Profit) would this information best fit, and how could it be restructured?'

Remember, the more context you provide, the better the output you'll receive. Repeat this process with all the Sections that you need to restructure.

Tools & Resources

It's now time to list the Tools & Resources. You can use a prompt like this in ChatGPT to request a list of tools and resources for each category: 'Please provide a list of tools and resources that could be helpful for each of the following Categories in the context of a [restaurant] franchise operations manual? The Categories are:

1. Introduction

2. New Business Setup & Support

3. People (Your Team)

4. Marketing & Promotion

5. Day-to-Day Operating Requirements

6. Business Development, Growth & Profit

For example, in the Marketing & Promotion category, useful tools and resources could include brand guidelines, brand elements and marketing tools such as a marketing programme and calendar.'

This prompt outlines the task clearly and provides an example of what you're seeking. You can adjust the wording to suit your needs.

In the Core Operating Brand Standards Manual, the Tools & Resources will be hyperlinked individually to a knowledge-sharing environment such as Microsoft SharePoint, a knowledge-sharing centre such as a franchisee portal, or a knowledge-sharing platform. When the franchisee clicks on the link, the tool or resource will open in a separate window.

Use your smartphone camera to capture the *Manual Magic* Library QR code to unlock typical Tools & Resources for Marketing & Promotion.

manualmagic.manual.to/**library**

Collaboration

When you have created the Sections and Topics, confirm they flow logically and are intuitive for the reader. Ask all stakeholders to collaborate so everyone can provide input to the resulting Structure & Contents. Obtain feedback on the areas where further clarification might be needed as well as any redundancies or gaps.

Use these insights to ensure that you've structured the information in a manner that's effective for the franchisee. This refined outline will serve as your Structure & Contents blueprint for a clearer, more comprehensive Operations Manual:

- Keep stakeholders in the loop, receive and implement feedback with comments, and customise document access so you can all work from a single source of truth.

- Organise an in-person team meeting where everyone brainstorms the Sections and Topics using a whiteboard or flipchart.

- Organise a Zoom meeting to brainstorm the topics using the integrated Whiteboard program. This is where your team works together in real time. You can share any document with your colleagues, regardless of device or physical location.

- Use Fathom in Zoom apps to record, transcribe, highlight and summarise the meeting so you can focus on the conversation.

- Use physical, coloured cards. Many solopreneurs prefer this method when working independently. This is because you can move the Sections and Topics around to form a logical order. Use different colours according to the hierarchy.

Five standard headings

When you believe your Structure & Contents is as complete as you can make it, you will need to add five standard headings to the beginning of every Section of your Structure & Contents. These are:

- Introduction (setting the context)
- Minimum Operating Standards

- Roles & Responsibilities

- Measure, Analyse, Improve

- Tools & Resources (discussed in Tools & Resources above)

Standard headings create a consistent format and structure throughout the manual:

- They make it easier for franchisees to navigate and locate relevant information quickly.

- They ensure that each section covers essential aspects of the topic, providing franchisees with a clear understanding of the requirements, expectations and procedures.

- When franchisees become familiar with the standardised format, they can quickly find and process information, enabling them to perform tasks and make decisions more efficiently.

For information on how to create the five headings, see Chapter 7, Underpinning The Franchise Agreement.

A final gap analysis

When you believe your Structure & Contents is as complete as you can make it, you should perform a gap analysis. Take your franchise agreement and go through every line in minute detail, checking off every term and condition in the agreement to ensure that the Topics have been covered off in your draft Structure & Contents. If applicable, take your business and marketing plan and make sure that your Structure & Contents also aligns with your current and future plans. When you're satisfied the Sections and Topics faithfully represent your Business System this will become the Structure & Contents template for content creation.

Summary

- The franchise agreement, business plan and marketing collateral are the main tools to draw up your Structure & Contents.

- Whatever publication format you choose, the Categories identified will work well to organise your IP.

- Create Sections and Topics with the assistance of AI.

- Use AI to help reverse-outline and upgrade your current Operations Manual.

- Create digital and hard copy formats so you can keep track of what you've included in your Structure & Contents.

- Always perform a gap analysis when you have created a final draft Structure & Contents.

4
Drawing Up Your Project Plan

A plan is the yeast that makes success rise. Similarly, the Project Plan is the yeast that helps your success rise. Without it, your Operations Manual, much like a yeast-less cake, may turn out dense and unappealing, failing to rise to the occasion.

The art of baking and project planning are remarkably similar; both require precision, patience and the perfect recipe or plan to succeed. Drawing up your Project Plan is like assembling the ingredients for a cake. Just as a baker needs the right elements for a recipe, the Project Plan outlines the tasks, activities, and procedures required to complete your Operations Manual.

Creating a franchise Operations Manual is a complex project that involves many moving parts. The Project

Coordinator must ensure transparency about the process and expectations and communicate clearly with all involved parties.

By the end of this chapter, you will:

- Understand the features and benefits of a Project Plan.

- Learn how to set realistic deadlines and manage, create and deliver your manual.

- Understand why you must keep your plan up to date.

- Use your smartphone camera to capture the *Manual Magic* Library QR code to access additional Tools & Resources.

The Project Plan

The Project Plan supports strategic and long-range planning, much as yeast works throughout the baking process. It might seem small and insignificant initially, but it's critical in matching short-term and long-term goals with specific solutions.

Think of your Project Plan as a detailed recipe, helping to ensure that the project, like a cake, is baked from concept to completion efficiently and effectively. It's the baker's guide to timing, temperature and techniques, leading to a perfectly baked cake – in your case, a successful Operations Manual. You need one regardless of whether you're managing the project independently or with your team.

Scope

The scope is based on the detailed Structure & Contents – the blueprint of your Business System created in Chapter 3. It defines the project's objectives and deliverables, outlining the work required from individual stakeholders to achieve your goals. It determines these critical functions:

- The type of content you will need to create – eg, text, video, audio, infographics.

- Critical tasks and milestones – eg, first, second and final drafts, multimedia elements created, sign-off, production and publication.

- The content owner(s) – ie, the stakeholders who will provide the content.

- Designer(s), if appropriate.

- IT support.

- The user-friendly knowledge-sharing environment you've chosen for your franchise's stage of maturity – eg, cloud-based, franchisee portal/intranet, knowledge-sharing platform; this will take into consideration the plan for today and in two to five years' time.

- Timelines.

- Costs.

Checklist

Use this checklist to ensure that you are including all the necessary steps for a successful Project Plan:

- List the specific tasks, activities or procedures necessary to complete the project, broken down into manageable units.

- Establish the start and end dates for each task and the overall project, ensuring that resources are allocated appropriately.

- Identify the personnel required to complete the project, helping to avoid bottlenecks and delays.

- Estimate the costs associated with each task and the overall project, allowing for proper financial planning and management.

- Identify potential risks and outline strategies to mitigate them, ensuring a smoother project execution.

- Establish standards and processes to monitor and maintain quality throughout the project.

- Define the channels and methods of communication between stakeholders, ensuring clear and timely information exchange.

Benefits

A clear and well-defined Project Plan allows for optimal resource allocation and streamlines work processes by defining the tasks and resources required:

- It facilitates communication among stakeholders – eg, team members and franchisees. It minimises misunderstandings and ensures that everyone is on the same page.

- It enables team members to understand their roles and responsibilities, promoting a collaborative work environment.

- It reduces project failure by identifying potential risks and outlining mitigation strategies.

- It helps maintain financial control and avoids overspending by estimating project costs and tracking expenditure.

- A clear timeline helps prioritise tasks and ensure the project is completed on schedule.

Drawing up the plan

The Project Coordinator works with stakeholders to establish project objectives, scope and deliverables. They then develop a detailed plan that outlines tasks, resources, timelines and budgets. The Project Coordinator tracks the progress of each task, ensuring that it's completed on time and within budget. They also manage any issues or risks that arise during the project.

The travel contingencies mentioned in Chapter 2, such as the unexpected detour through Turkey, mirror the potential issues you might encounter while creating your manual. You may encounter missing data, change in franchise operations or the need for revisions. In these cases, having a contingency plan helps you keep your project on track, as it did on the trip.

The frequency of updates to the Project Plan depends on the project's complexity and duration. The Project Coordinator should review and update the Project Plan at least every month, ensuring it remains relevant and continues to reflect any project scope, resources or timeline changes. If timescales slip, the Project Coordinator should:

- **Identify the cause:** Determine the reasons behind the delay and assess the impact on the project.

- **Re-evaluate the plan:** Adjust the timeline, resources or tasks as needed to address the delay and minimise its impact on the project.

- **Communicate with stakeholders:** Inform stakeholders of the delay, the reasons behind it and the steps taken to address it. This maintains transparency and trust.

To manage a project successfully, I would recommend using a tracking tool. This could be a project management tool such as MS Project or you could build a Gantt Chart in Excel.

Setting realistic deadlines

Don't set up yourself or your team members to fail. Setting realistic deadlines for the creation and delivery of your Operations Manual is fundamental to ensure that the manual is comprehensive, accurate and useful for franchisees. The basis of your Project Plan is the Structure & Contents – this is your Business System Blueprint.

The first step is to fully comprehend the extent of the project. What are the required sections and elements in the Operations Manual? What's the level of detail needed? Who are the intended readers? Answering these questions will help you establish a clear picture of the work ahead:

- **Key milestones:** Your key milestones are the Categories, Sections, Tools & Resources, and other elements such as drafts, multimedia creation, sign-off, formatting, design, printing and uploading. Each should have a clear start and end point.

- **Assign responsibilities:** Stakeholders should have clear instructions on their role and understand the project's goals. You will need to define who is responsible for creating each

Section of the manual. It may be an internal team member, your IT specialist, a designer or a professional editor. Their initials should be noted against the element(s) assigned, with deadlines for delivery of, say, the first draft, second draft and final draft of the Core Operating Brand Standards Manual (COBSM) through sign-off. As an element passes through from concept to completion, it can be highlighted in yellow.

- **Task duration:** Work collaboratively with the assigned individuals to estimate how long each task should take. Remember, it's better to overestimate and deliver early than underestimate and miss the deadline. This estimation should consider the research, drafting, editing and reviewing stages.

- **Project timeline:** Based on the task duration, develop a project timeline. This timeline should be sequential and visual, clearly showing the expected start and completion dates for each task.

- **Regular check-ins:** Schedule regular check-ins to ensure that the project is on track. These are opportunities to address problems, revise estimates and update the timeline if necessary.

- **Set buffer time:** Always set aside some buffer time for unforeseen challenges, revisions or changes in project scope. This could be a percentage of the total project time or a set number of days or weeks.

- **Allow the deliverables to flow:** Establish a rolling programme of content delivery, editing the draft and signing off content ready for publication.

- **Final review and revision:** After all text sections of the COBSM have been drafted, and all additional tools and resources created, time must be allocated for comprehensive review, feedback and revisions. This ensures the document is coherent, accurate and meets the needs of your franchisees.

- **Approval and delivery:** Once the COBSM has been reviewed and finalised, and all additional tools and resources created, time must be allocated for final approvals and preparation of the elements for production. This could include formatting, design, printing, converting to pdfs, and uploading.

- **Project evaluation:** After the project is completed, evaluate what went well and what didn't. This feedback can help improve the process for future projects.

Summary

- Regardless of whether you are managing the project independently or with a team, a Project Plan is essential.

- The Project Plan enables you to keep the development of all Operations Manual elements on track.

- On completion, evaluate what went well and what didn't so that you can adjust the process accordingly.

5
Patisserie Pénélope – Our Case Study

Patisserie Pénélope is the fictional case study that forms the basis for my Structure & Contents workshops. It's the story of a retail franchise which launched with a hard copy of its Operations Manual, went digital and, with a growing network, embraced the concept of knowledge sharing.

The information illustrated via this case study addresses many of the elements that must come together to create a detailed Structure & Contents – the blueprint of the business model and system.

Use your smartphone camera to capture the *Manual Magic* QR code and unlock additional materials.

manualmagic.manual.to/library

Individual or team exercise

You can use this case study for an individual or team exercise. For example, choose Marketing & Promotion to build your Structure & Contents:

- Identify Sections (ie, the processes) based on this case study.

- Place the Sections in a logical order.

- Choose one Section and develop a list of Topics representing the procedure(s).

- Create a Standard Operating Procedure (SOP) for that Section.

- List the Tools & Resources to underpin that Section. These may include brand identity guidelines and elements such as logo, font and colour. Include checklists, formwork, examples of press releases and advertisements, stock images, supplier lists, etc.

- Develop brand guidelines.

Case study concept

I chose Patisserie Pénélope for my case study because it relates to early childhood memories of my mother's homemade cakes. Her passion was baking the most delicious cakes and pastries for when I came home from school.

It's Friday afternoon, and my father has collected me for the two-week half-term holiday from school 50 miles away. I'm standing in the hallway, setting down my heavy satchel filled with holiday homework on the old monk's bench. Mother, in her Robert Carrier apron, wipes her floured hands on it as she leaves the kitchen to greet me. The aroma of home baking is everywhere. My excitement rises. I walk the few short steps into the kitchen and find chocolate and coffee éclairs on the kitchen countertop, some waiting to be filled from my mother's piping bag. I can almost taste the chocolate icing and the crème pâtissière as it oozes out.

Mille-feuilles, doughnuts, and tarts filled with fruit from our kitchen garden are cooling on the blue Formica table, which matches our modern, early Sixties-style Dainty Maid kitchen. A just-opened package reveals two pots of clotted Cornish cream, thick enough to stand a spoon up straight, which my mother has ordered specially. What a treat! My sweet tooth, so delightfully trained, has never left me: home-baked bread and croissants, pastries and sausage rolls. Who can resist them?

Then there were the birthday cakes and others ordered for special occasions from Elisabeth the Chef[6] – the first company in the Midlands area of the UK to introduce continental patisserie-type products onto the market. Founded in 1928 by Mr and Mrs Chesterfield, by 1976, they were operating twelve company-owned retail outlets and supplying twenty major high-class stores before franchising reached the UK. An early strapline read: 'Near or far… give them the taste of home.'

When I lived in London's fashionable Knightsbridge in the Seventies, Maison Verlon opened on Pavilion Road, SW1, around the corner from Harrods – next to the laundrette I used weekly. So, the temptation was close at hand. The owners, Vera and Leon, became dear friends. At the close of business on Saturdays, I would take the lift to my sixth-floor apartment armed with boxes filled to the brim with Viennese pastries. Little wonder I could see myself running a patisserie in my mind's eye.

Single-unit franchise

Today the retail franchise, Patisserie Pénélope, that I could so easily have launched is purely imaginary. In my mind's eye, my franchisees create the same

---

6   R Sheppard, 'Where high quality is a moral ingredient', *Baker's Review* (6 March 1970), www.elisabeth-the-chef.co.uk/ ETCBakersReview.pdf, accessed 6 July 2023

bastions of delight from my mother's repertoire and we now bake muffins and sourdough bread, which have become so trendy.

It's a single-unit franchise – the basic form of franchise – where the franchisor grants a franchisee the right to open and operate one franchise unit. Yet, it offers multi-unit growth opportunities. There are plans for global expansion.

High Street locations are chosen for their high visibility and the best footfall. Whenever possible, the sites are near easy parking and transport. This makes access as easy as possible for customers. There are plans to open twenty more stores in shopping malls and airports over the next two years.

Consumers love the irresistible smell of fresh coffee to take out with a cake or newly-baked loaf as they approach and enter the spotlessly clean store. In the window is a bountiful, well-merchandised display of bread, delicious cakes and mouth-watering pastries at competitive prices by which passers-by are tempted.

Our culture

The Patisserie Pénélope culture is about the name and recognising, like Elisabeth the Chef and Maison Verlon, that 'high quality is a moral ingredient'. In Greek mythology, Pénélope was the wife of Ulysses, known for being faithful and loyal – in modern times, devoted to her business model and, of course, her customers. By customers, we mean our internal and external customers – our franchisees and our consumers.

I was named after Penny Craig, the younger of three sisters played by Deanna Durbin in *Three Smart Girls*, the 1936 musical comedy. My mother had fallen in love with the character. Only 'proper' names could be registered when I was born, so although my legal name is Pénélope – hence Patisserie Pénélope – I've always been 'Penny'.

The nickname Penny is associated with being cheerful and energetic. Here, this means cheerfully delivering the perfect customer experience – each time, every time – and giving the customer more than expected 'The Patisserie Pénélope Way'.

Success comes from caring about what we do and doing it professionally. Our core purpose is to deliver 'Delight in Every Bite'. That means delivering more than expected to delight our customers so that they become brand advocates and, ultimately, 'Raving Fans'. Therefore, all our franchisees must deliver consistency in their business.

Consistency covers everything from the staff we recruit and the training we provide, to the products we sell and how our franchisees deliver excellence.

It's no exaggeration to say that the strength of our network depends on everyone operating their franchises consistently to the standards we set within the legal framework of the franchise agreement and all local legal and regulatory requirements. The brand and our collective profits suffer if the chain has one weak link.

Our promise and focus

The Patisserie Pénélope service promise and values go back to medieval times when bakers were members of the English guild system. When they joined their guilds, bakers signed an oath promising not to cheat customers of money or goods when purchasing or selling them. So, our franchise's core values are honesty and integrity. We promise to delight every customer with an extra item to try – free of charge – with every order of four or more purchased. It's a fun way to treat customers. But there's more to it than that and the name. It enables counter service staff to upsell to increase sales by tempting customers into buying more goods.

- Customers come first – always – because customers can choose what they buy and from who.

- Quality is critical to success.

- Teamwork is our strength.

New Business Setup & Support

We welcome franchisees to our growing network of passionate and dedicated franchise owners. A franchisee is not an entrepreneurial twin, but needs and wants to follow our Business System.

A Patisserie Pénélope franchisee can take pride in being part of a dynamic, innovative brand committed to delivering exceptional experiences to its customers and supporting the success of its franchise network. As an ethical franchisor, we provide a strong foundation for the franchised business, offering a wide range of support services, resources and growth opportunities to help franchisees succeed.

The Patisserie Pénélope Franchise Package aims to create a strong foundation for the franchised business and foster a long-lasting, successful partnership. It offers franchisees a comprehensive and well-rounded support system, addressing all aspects of launching, operating and growing a successful franchise. By providing comprehensive support, training and resources, Patisserie Pénélope ensures that franchisees have access to everything they need to achieve success in their local markets.

With our commitment to their success, they can confidently embark on this exciting journey and build a successful Patisserie Pénélope franchise, creating exceptional products and experiences for customers while positively impacting their community.

By partnering with Patisserie Pénélope, they are joining a brand committed to excellence and innovation. Together, we will continue to elevate the Patisserie Pénélope brand and provide exceptional experiences to our valued customers.

People (Our Team)

We believe in recruiting franchisees (and their team members) with the right traits, characteristics and attitudes. This enables the network to deliver planned and spontaneous 'Wows' to our customers through true teamwork.

After trading successfully, proving the concept and embedding the franchise systems with two pilot franchises over 18 months, our growing bakery franchise has thirty stores in prime locations. Each franchise is operated by a carefully recruited owner/manager who matches our franchisee profile and can build a solid team around them to deliver our products and services to our minimum quality standards.

Team members must carry out their roles with passion, enthusiasm, confidence and outstanding execution. Because of Brexit, the type of worker we used to employ is no longer available, so our recruitment process must adapt to the few people we can still find in today's talent pool. That means our team member profile tends to be younger, from diverse backgrounds, and often without the right qualifications or skills. As we look further for those team members, we also need to accept that they may not be English-speaking. Taking their learning preferences into consideration is of paramount importance for successful onboarding and integration. Moreover, meeting their needs, speaking their language and making them feel confident are critical factors in reducing employee turnover.

Most owners/managers need more business management experience when recruited. Our franchisee profile requires them to be insightful, quick learners, capable of dealing with difficult situations, caring about people and creating an environment that respects sustainability. Our owners/managers:

- Question statements, challenge opinions and carefully evaluate conclusions. They accept and learn from their mistakes and increase their self-awareness.

- Are flexible and creative and demonstrate problem-solving skills, which are vital when running a business.

- Ensure that team members – the manager, head bakers, kitchen hands and counter-service staff – share the character traits, behaviours and attributes that fit our purpose, vision, and culture.

At any time, there must be sufficient team members to operate the franchise efficiently and profitably.

The patisserie's training academy delivers brand, management, skills training and ongoing training to ensure a firm foundation and develop each business. Key to this is learning how to use Patisserie Pénélope's brand guidelines and maintain a consistent visual identity for their business so that all employees know how to present our brand, themselves and their store to the public. No franchisee can operate their new business without successfully passing brand induction and the initial training programme.

Our new bakers undergo brand induction and the bakery's rigorous kitchen skills training; customer-facing staff are trained in essential selling skills. Central to all activities are health, safety and food hygiene.

The staff love brand induction, as they get to sample the different types of sourdough bread, cakes and regional specialities during this and the skills training programme. This takes place at our head office premises with its fully operational patisserie – the original flagship store upon which the franchise concept was rolled out. Specific brand and initial training are fundamental, but the key to employee loyalty is offering development training and a career path, allowing team members to reach their ultimate career objectives and goals.

Marketing & Promotion

Regardless of where a patisserie is located, it's instantly recognisable. Customers feel comfortable and safe in the eye-catching shades of appetising pinks, lip-smacking browns, tempting oranges and fresh blues. The large, distinctive PP logo encircled by our full name – Patisserie Pénélope – depicted in the 'Fabrica bold' font is etched into the storefront glass. Below is our tagline: 'Delight in Every Bite'. This stands out beautifully against the eye-catching brown, orange and green décor – just the colours to get those taste-buds jumping! At the point of sale, daily and monthly promotions are posted on the menu board, which window shoppers can read easily.

Customer-facing staff are perfectly presented in their bright, green, pressed workwear with logo and name badge so customers can address them personally. They greet each customer warmly with a genuine, welcoming smile and a cheery, 'Good morning/good afternoon,' remembering their regulars' names.

There's a national promotional calendar to which all franchisees gear the marketing in their territory. They also participate in their territory's local events, such as fêtes and charity events. The franchise manager arranges 'By invitation only' special tasting evenings for new products. These are always oversubscribed by customers. Events generate plenty of PR opportunities for the local press and supplement a seasonally planned schedule of advertisements strategically placed in local and regional media.

We never have to worry that our franchisees are off-brand or will respond incorrectly to a social media post. We take the initiative in reputation management with centralised support by providing social media campaigns, photos, videos and posts as a service to all franchisees. Content is published on Facebook, Instagram, Twitter, or LinkedIn to local office social media audiences. We use Head Office to franchise network, using a one-to-many social media content publishing system[7] to get social media right every time. This provides us with publishing control for the brand, saves time, increases efficiency and gives us greater control of our brand voice and messages. It also enables us to acquire intelligence on our social media strategy. It's quick and easy to set up and costs less than the price of a Mars Bar a day for each participating franchisee.

Customers receive the same warm welcome and enjoy the same high-quality products sold by a small friendly team who have created a happy and harmonious environment. Our EPOS system is integrated across the network, so customers pay without the hassle and payments are uploaded at the end of the day.

---

7   https://socialhandler.online

The counter staff are skilled at selling the bakery's products. They know the ingredients of every product – which ones are gluten-free and which contain lactose or nuts. They cannot afford to get this wrong if a customer has an allergy. Staff are proud of the products they sell and, by our 'baker's dozen 4 + 1' promotion, often manage to persuade the customer to try something extra, thereby increasing the value of the sale.

Customers leave the bakery looking forward to their next visit; purchases are placed carefully in our unique pastry packaging. These are specially designed cardboard cake boxes, wrappers and carrier bags with the bakery's corporate logo, local phone number and opening times advertised prominently.

All new customer contact details are captured with the necessary data protection consent at the point of sale and added to the bakery's email list. Each bakery enjoys a strong core of loyal customers who need to be – and like being – nurtured. They look forward to their regular visits and love receiving the monthly newsletter introducing special offers and recipes with a voucher for a new product to try on their next visit. Our Recipe of the Month can be accessed using a QR code printed on the back cover of our newsletter, pointing to a URL. Scanning the QR code with their smartphone immediately takes them to the public recipe section of our knowledge-sharing platform.

Finding loyal customers who recommend the bakery to all their friends is immensely satisfying. So, the bakery acquires more customers to serve who become great brand advocates, which means acquiring them doesn't cost any more. The challenge is to turn them into 'Raving Fans for Life'.

Day-to-Day Operating Requirements

The skilled bakers across the franchisee network collectively bake thousands of loaves weekly. They know how to cut the dough to the correct size/weight first time, every time. Our signature loaf has two secret ingredients – pure pine water and love. Cakes and pastries are made to the same core recipes.

The top-quality ingredients are locally sourced whenever possible. The kitchen hand supports them in producing different types of sourdough loaves, cakes and pastries to the same recipes daily. Specials are baked at all the important festivals – eg, Easter, Eid, Diwali and Christmas. Bakers also make celebration cakes to order. A lot is happening, so there's no time or place for errors.

Bakers work long hours, generally beginning work at around 04.00 hours – earlier before significant holidays – ready to open for business at 08.00 hours, Monday to Saturday. The manager and service staff arrive an hour before opening to ensure that the contract cleaning staff have cleaned and sanitised all customer areas such as the entrance, floor, counter surfaces and display areas, and that they are debris-free. They also check that the service counter is laid out correctly – eg, supplies of sugar, stirrers and serviettes are fully replenished – before the bread and pastries are brought out by the kitchen hand to merchandise to the store planogram in time to receive the day's customers.

Baking is physically demanding. Kneading dough, lifting heavy bags of flour and standing for 8-12 hours a day can be exhausting. Bakers must be physically fit and robust; those heavy bags of flour don't lift themselves! And although many bakers work in a warm, oven-heated environment, they frequently go to cold storage to retrieve ingredients or store perishable products. However, seeing customers' faces light up when they take home a loaf of bread that you made or a perfect cake that you baked makes all the effort worthwhile. While working in a bakery can be physically demanding, there are advantages, such as the varied tasks performed and the chance to use creativity when decorating cakes.

Suitable clothing and shoes are essential. All staff must be perfectly presented, with long hair in a net, nails trimmed, and a single wedding ring as appropriate.

The staff arrive early to sanitise their station surface before assembling the ingredients for the day's bread, pastries and cakes. Products containing nuts are prepped in a dedicated area. Bakers, ably supported by one or more kitchen hands depending on bakery size, consult the list for the day and assemble the ingredients and utensils needed so that each loaf, cake or pastry will be baked to the same standard of excellence as those baked the day before – and will be the day after.

If a new baker needs refresher training – eg, to follow all or part of a recipe, especially a regional speciality – they can instantly access and process the recipe by scanning the equivalent QR code with their smartphone. This leads them to a series of brief video snippets with accompanying text in their language. The videos can be created between team members and approved by the manager and Head Office.

At least one team member has been trained as a barista. The barista ensures our rich, roasted Italian takeaway coffee is freshly ground and perfectly tamped. The cappuccino milk, with dairy and dairy-free options, is heated to the exact temperature necessary to obtain the correct quantity and density of froth. Each cup is topped off with the PP Patisserie Pénélope logo depicted in the customer's choice of chocolate or cinnamon sprinkles. The counter staff serve a range of takeaway traditional and herbal teas, too.

A new barista can scan a QR code and quickly learn how to brew and present the perfect coffee. They know that if the milk is burned, the foam will disappear and the coffee will be bitter. This increases complaints and leads to refunds and wastage. Every team member understands that wastage erodes profits.

Teamwork, collaboration and engagement

Many staff have been with their bakery since the franchise was launched fifteen years ago. They feel valued and motivated. We know that soft skills are essential.

Effective communication is crucial in any team. It ensures that everyone understands their roles and responsibilities and it fosters a harmonious work environment. In a patisserie franchise, communication skills help with passing instructions, discussing recipes and managing customer relations.

A patisserie franchise is a teamwork-driven environment where bakers, front-of-house staff and managers must collaborate effectively. Teamwork skills are necessary for ensuring smooth operations, from baking and decorating pastries to selling them to customers.

Problems can arise in any business. The ability to think critically, identify problems, and come up with effective solutions is vital. In a patisserie, problem-solving involves tackling a recipe that isn't working, dealing with equipment breakdowns or resolving conflicts between staff.

The food industry is fast-paced and constantly changing. Being adaptable allows a team member to handle unexpected situations, adjust to changes in customer demands or market trends and learn new techniques or recipes quickly.

Effective leadership is vital in guiding the team towards achieving our goals. It involves making strategic decisions, inspiring and motivating the team and ensuring that the franchise consistently delivers the perfect customer experience.

While having these soft skills is beneficial, it's also important to foster an environment where these skills are appreciated and nurtured. This contributes to the overall success of the patisserie franchise.

Every Monday at 08.00 hours, the franchise manager holds a team briefing to review the previous week's trading and to discuss any issues. These are noted on the system so that Head Office can identify any emerging trends across the network – eg, accidents from poor manual handling or customer complaints about the cleanliness of the stores.

The franchise manager holds scheduled monthly team briefings, setting the agenda a few days prior. Team members are encouraged to suggest how to run the business more effectively. If taken up by the franchisor as best practice and rolled out across the network, the top suggestions will be announced at the annual conference and the Franchise of the Year Awards in the 'best practice contribution' category. The franchise manager and their team member will be recognised and rewarded. Every quarter, the team meets for a review over supper, paid for by their store.

Mary, a team member, had been with one of our top performing franchises for only a few months when she approached her franchise manager and said,

> 'I've noticed that Sam, our apprentice kitchen hand, keeps forgetting to take the butter out of the fridge before using it. We both know that if the butter is too cold, the sugar can't penetrate it and air pockets can't form. This results in uneven bakes. Cold butter is also hopeless for making buttercream frosting. So, he then puts the butter in the microwave, which makes it too warm and liquid. Using it also ruins the cakes and leads to wastage, because they are dense and uneven. They shouldn't be offered for sale. When they are, we get complaints, so we need to start the batch again. On average, we're spoiling one batch in twenty every month.'

Mary had worked out that to avoid this, the butter needed to be taken out of the fridge two hours in advance. However, when that wasn't possible, she had also figured out the best, quickest and most effective way to soften one kilo of butter at a time for making cakes or buttercream frosting using the microwave.

The franchise manager encouraged Mary to use her smartphone to make a video clip for each stage of the butter softening process, starring Sam and making sure not to record his face or any identifying characteristics. They didn't need to write and memorise a script, because they wouldn't be adding a voiceover.[8] Then it was a simple process of adding short text to the video clips. (Optionally, these texts could have been made from text to speech and could also have been translated into the most used languages using AI.) Mary created the accompanying texts by typing out the steps to match each video clip:

1. Inspect the microwave. It must be clean. Otherwise, clean it before use.

2. Spray the kitchen surface you will be using with antibacterial Sanitec and dry it with a disposable kitchen wipe, disposing of it in the designated bin.

3. Thoroughly wash your hands in hot water for 20 seconds using the antibacterial soap provided. Scan the QR code in this case study for an example of best practice.

---

8   Note: Video with voiceover is good for building rapport and when you need to convey emotion – for example, in brand marketing or when explaining how an accident happened and how to avoid it. However, it's not that efficient for instructions and usually takes about ten times longer to produce. In addition, the pitch, speed and quality will differ for each instruction, reducing uniformity. Some people speak too slowly, others too fast and others prefer different paces. Similarly, if they talk with a heavy accent or aren't native language speakers, they can be hard to understand. It can also be unsafe should a team member rely solely on audio without video. You need a lot of takes on a voiceover, but you only need one or two takes for a visual action.

manualmagic.manual.to/**washinghands**

4. Dry your hands using the kitchen dryer. Its HEPA filters are designed to trap germs and blow only clean air.

5. Take a clean, deep microwave glass dish from the cupboard to hold a kilo of cold butter easily.

6. Set the dish firmly on the sanitised surface.

7. Open the fridge and take out 4 x 250gram portions of unsalted butter.

8. Carefully unwrap one pat of butter at a time, leaving it in the wrapper.

9. Take the knife with a 14cm blade from the kitchen knife rack.

10. Run the hot tap until the water becomes hot enough to touch, being careful not to scald yourself.

11. Place the blade under the running water to make the butter easy to cut, counting slowly to thirty.

12. Shake the excess water from the edge before slicing each portion.

13. Be careful to keep the blade away so as not to cut yourself.

14. Cut across the width of the portion to make eight equal slices.

15. Cut once across the centre of the portion length to make sixteen small butter pats.

16. Without touching the butter, pick up each portion in its wrapper and turn the butter into a microwavable dish.

17. Fold the wrapper into two, butter side in. Dispose of the wrapper in the bin provided.

18. Repeat for all four portions.

19. Open the microwave door and place the dish on the shelf in the centre of the microwave.

20. Shut the door firmly until you hear it click.

21. Using the lowest power setting, set the timer for one 5-second increment.

22. Check that the butter is beginning to soften.

23. Set the timer for another 5-second increment, observing progress through the safety glass door.

24. Unless liquid butter is required for a different recipe, don't let the butter separate into a thin foam, butter fat, milk solids and water.

25. Stop the microwave when the butter is creamy, but hasn't melted completely.

26. If the butter needs more time to soften, set the timer again on the lowest setting for another 5-second increment.

27. Remove the hot bowl using the oven gloves located on the hook nearby.

28. Carefully set down the bowl on the kitchen surface.

29. Take a clean plastic spatula from the rack and, holding the bowl firmly, gently stir the softened butter until it's smooth and creamy.

30. Immediately take the ready-to-use, softened butter over to the baker.

Creating this instruction took about 45 minutes, with only one retake to record the thirty video snippets and to add the accompanying text into the online instructions editor using her smartphone. With her manager's approval, this instruction was shared with Head Office.

We were so impressed by Mary's initiative. We reviewed the video snippets in our knowledge-sharing platform's kitchen operations section, made minor edits, approved them, published them and generated the QR code. This took a matter of minutes. We then made the new instruction available to the entire network – instantly.

All kitchen hands can now use their smartphones to capture this QR code or find the instruction in the knowledge base and follow Mary's instructions with texts in their native language at the time and point of need. If, for example, we later change the manufacturer of the sanitiser, Mary merely re-records that step with Sam, and we change the name of the sanitiser in the accompanying text.

Mary is immensely proud to see that her instructions have been added for everyone to use, and was delighted, of course, when she received a store gift voucher as her reward. Sam is thrilled to feature in the work instruction, although he's not pictured recognisably. Within the hour, Mary and Sam had received positive feedback. 'Hey, I love what you did there,' Josh, the head baker from another franchise territory, texted. 'That's great. It will save me time, and the butter will be perfect for our Victoria sponges.'

Across the network, we have reduced wastage for all the recipes requiring softened butter to 0.2% down from about 7%. There are no customer complaints about the stodgy cakes anymore and our bakers are very happy with their butter softened to the correct consistency.

Spurred on by this success, Mary, of course, is now fully engaged in continuous improvement. What's more, she now shares her experience with her colleagues, encouraging them to seek improvements so that they can also recommend more effective methods of working for the benefit of the network. They are all now competing against each other for next year's franchise conference and the franchisee of the year awards.

It's a win-win all around. We see a quick return on our investment. When we used to create the simple picture- and text-based procedures, we often felt like we were pouring money down the drain and investing in something that wouldn't be used. The creator gets a quick positive feedback loop. Team members are now proud to share their know-how.

Checklists

Managers use a series of store checklists on our knowledge-sharing platform, accessed via smartphones. Checklists enable franchisees and their teams to stay organised and productive – eg, internal and external cleaning and daily store opening and closing checklists. As each task is checked off, a button changes from red to green so we can monitor those franchisees who have completed the self-audit and provide additional support for those who don't.

Team members are encouraged to play an active role in achieving the KPIs we set for each franchise each month and are keen to reach or exceed the targets we set for the network.

The manager always orders top-quality ingredients from the same, reliable quality-checked suppliers we have approved by our strict quality control criteria. Deliveries must arrive at each store in perfect condition on time, every time, ready to be checked off against an online purchase order. Ingredients must be stored immediately in ideal conditions, monitored and recorded in the system.

Supplies are ordered through our bespoke software program. Bakers keep a watchful eye on supplies and use the FIFO (First In, First Out) method of stock rotation and control, ensuring that the newest delivery of ingredients and coffee are stored at the back, moving the oldest to the front.

Franchisees know that wastage, along with poor machinery maintenance and measurement, is the enemy of the store's bottom line. Accidentally add too much sugar? There goes the batter that would have made a dozen cakes.

Teaching the team how to monitor leftovers is essential to the franchise manager's brief. Tracking leftovers is how they know there's too much of one product, so they can adjust by cutting back or eliminating an unpopular line.

Development, Growth & Profit

Our systems are designed to make it easy for our franchisees to be successful and profitable, unencumbered by hugely time-consuming administration.

Management service fees based on the monthly turn-over are calculated automatically and payments are remitted by the due date. We also collect the 2% levy for national marketing.

Forecasting sales accurately allows the franchisee to plan inventory, create a baking schedule and adjust marketing. Monitoring sales patterns and complaints across the network can reveal insights about products, service and customer satisfaction that might otherwise be missed. A mystery shopper programme is an essential aspect of assuring customer satisfaction.

Each franchise is compared with the others and against competitors in their territory or region every quarter. New franchisees can expect quarterly business development visits until they've traded successfully for 18 months. Established franchisees receive one business development visit yearly, unless more is requested or necessary.

An annual audit of the entire operation, including brand management, is conducted every year for each franchise. A traffic light system based on the Balanced Scorecard[9] is the basis of the audit. When I helped them develop their initial manuals, this is the strategic planning and management system that

---

9   The Balanced Scorecard management system, https://balancedscorecard.org/bsc-basics-overview

Whitbread plc used for their Costa Coffee and Premier Inn brands to:

- Communicate what they wanted to accomplish.

- Align their day-to-day work with strategy.

- Prioritise projects, products and services.

- Measure and monitor their progress towards strategic targets.

Action points arising from the audit must be completed within seven days (or longer by written agreement).

Support from Head Office is paramount, and all franchisees can contact their franchise support manager immediately if they need advice or guidance or have any concerns.

Operations Manual

The franchisor's know-how and its specialised processes, knowledge and proprietary information have been acquired through many years of experience – much of it learned the hard way. The Business System – the design, development and operation of all franchises – is set out in the Operations Manual. The manual sets out the minimum operating standards franchisees must meet so that, individually and collectively, success is achieved and the brand is developed.

Franchisees and their teams are encouraged to take ownership of their Operations Manual and discuss it with their franchise development manager during an annual audit and review. This ensures that content is up to date, relevant and continues to meet the needs of current and future franchisees.

Over the years, the Patisserie Pénélope Operations Manual has evolved from a hefty paper-based tome that few team members read into a password-protected, centralised knowledge-sharing platform. New technologies enable a manual to be developed more quickly and effectively in a far more engaging way than we ever thought possible. Now, we can see the number of user interactions for individual instructions and when a checklist is completed. We can see what's working and what's not – and update content in real time instead of waiting for the next update.

Hard copy

The original hard copy Operations Manual, issued to all franchisees on loan after signing the franchise agreement and just before training commenced, was cumbersome and difficult to read and use. It merely gathered dust on a shelf – except for the laminated recipes kept in the kitchen. You can guess the state these were in at the end of the baking shift!

It took forever to find what was needed. Just pages and pages of close type and text with few bullet points made reading tiring. No thought had been given to graphic white space or bullet points. All those headlines in capitals in bold with underlining and copious exclamation marks had put off readers entirely. Franchisees found this condescending.

Updates were a nightmare. Franchisees received a list with hard copies of the updated sheets to insert, swap and shred the out-of-date pages. Many franchisees shoved the new sheets into the front of the binder, which fell into a heap when the manual was taken down from the shelf. It became apparent that most franchisees weren't using their Operations Manual.

But they had a good guess at running the business after initial training, even if they received many customer complaints about the quality of our cakes and pastries or slow service delivery at peak times – especially when customers were queuing. Team members were often on sick leave with bad backs because they hadn't referred to instructions on how to lift sacks of flour and move heavy boxes of ingredients safely.

The time and costs of creating and printing the original Operations Manual were huge. It was disheartening to realise that the investment was mostly lost. Those days were when we were the sole fount of knowledge without a budget or access to professional guidance. As the franchise was small, it felt like a family; franchisees received a great deal of individual support.

Now that we are developing the network substantially, we don't have as much time to deal with operational queries. We realise that our approach to quality must change from being a 'franchise family' to operating a non-negotiable system – but a sufficiently flexible system to move with market forces. So, we adopted an 'iron fist in a velvet glove' approach to our Operations Manual to ensure uniformity and conformity across the network.

Cloud or portal

We then digitised the manual into a single pdf document and uploaded it to the cloud. Our options were Microsoft SharePoint or Dropbox, then a franchisee/ Intranet portal. We needed someone with the skill to create this complex document – to get the information out of an expert's brain, share it and get it inside a team member's head. In an ideal world, you will automatically transmit everything in your brain into a useable format for others to put back into their brains. But you can never capture everything in the brain. You will only capture a fraction of the expert's knowledge, even with skill.

Unfortunately, the content in pdf format quickly became outdated, requiring continuous updates, but with people unaware that there was an updated version. In time, we also realised that the traditional page format is not designed for smartphones and isn't readily translatable.

There are also more efficient ways to communicate information than plain text, as the younger generation, in particular, prefers video. Our workforce is changing, and these days, people want everything instantly. They want workplace instructions in short formats – eg, YouTube, Instagram and TikTok – produced by real people they identify with. They don't have the patience to wait to open their laptop, connect with a server and search for a specific recipe if they're in the middle of working with their hands covered in flour. They'll do it 'their way' instead of 'the right way'.

So, we appointed a small team of go-to experts to coach and mentor us on an effective and engaging way to deliver the manual. All franchisees were invited to participate in an anonymous online survey to bare their franchising souls and to take ownership of the manual's content. We optimised the blueprint of Patisserie Pénélope's Business System, organised our content, underpinned the franchise agreement's terms and conditions, and easily and quickly created engaging content to drive up efficiency.

Knowledge-sharing platform

Today, franchisees and their teams have password-protected access to our centralised, knowledge-sharing platform.[10] It is the fount of collective and collaborative knowledge about our franchise. From text-heavy content, we've moved to a self-serve content creation process that is immediately accessible and easier to exchange information. It significantly reduces the time and cost of manual creation and updating.

Information is more detailed, more effective and more efficient. We fully engage with our franchisees and their teams to create, share and update knowledge in their preferred language, which gives us a fast way to deliver behavioural change.

Our centralised, knowledge-sharing platform comprises a Core Operating Brand Standards Manual (COBSM). This text-heavy document underpins the terms and conditions of the franchise agreement as minimum standards. It sets out the franchisor's and franchisee's roles and responsibilities and how we will measure, analyse, and improve the business.

Using hyperlinks embedded in the text, or QR codes, the manual is underpinned by a comprehensive resource library of Tools & Resources: a multimedia database with video instructions to show franchisees how to set up and operate their business more efficiently daily – and to scale it.

Collectively, it has become the substance of our business model. It can be created and updated swiftly

---

10   https://manual.to

without the time and expense of producing a primarily text-based manual. This configuration helps franchisees replicate our patisserie Business System to our quality standards. It's a world away from the traditional hard copy manual.

QR codes

QR (Quick Resource) code stickers are generated through the knowledge-sharing platform and placed strategically throughout the workplace to enable team members to immediately access 'how-to' instructions in any language at the point of need. For example:

- A QR code sticker is placed on each coffee machine so the barista and other team members can strip down and clean them correctly.

- QR codes are placed in the storerooms to ensure that the kitchen hands and others safely handle heavy sacks of flour and boxes of ingredients.

- QR code stickers are used for many 'how-to' guides, from recipes to hygiene management, through brand management, customer service and refresher training.

Based on our brief and guidance, we invite team members to collaborate on a series of video snippets made with a smartphone that provides us with all our work instructions. Each complete video-based instruction can be shared as a QR code and the QR code always points to the latest version – eliminating the need to spend precious time accessing the manual online via a cloud-based system or franchisee portal to search for the relevant text.

Our team members, with different learning styles and needs, love creating and using these videos because it's a collaborative way to develop and learn, and they are proud of what they do.

Franchisees rarely need to consult the franchise support manager for information. This means we can spend more targeted time helping franchisees become successful and profitable.

Over the year during which we trialled the new Operations Manual format, there has been a noticeable improvement in uniformity and conformity across the network:

- Productivity and efficiency have increased, customer complaints have reduced and customer satisfaction has increased dramatically.

- We have acquired substantially more 'Raving Fans for Life'.

- Manual handling injuries have been reduced to zero since we recorded a video on how to lift heavy sacks of flour and other ingredients correctly.

Categories – the building blocks

Our know-how is categorised under these classic building blocks of a professional Operations Manual:

- **New Business Setup & Support:** This category offers comprehensive guidance on opening a new franchise, including information on location scouting, lease negotiation, store design, equipment purchasing and supplier relationships. It also provides support resources such as training programmes, and onboarding materials, and access to expert advice from the corporate team.

- **People (Your Team):** This category focuses on human resources and team management, covering topics like recruitment, hiring, onboarding, training, performance management and employee retention. It offers guidance on building a positive workplace culture and fostering employee engagement. Training includes managing your team to deliver the perfect customer experience – first time, every time – through a handpicked, motivated team.

- **Marketing & Promotion:** This category covers various aspects of marketing and promoting your franchise, including brand guidelines, local marketing strategies, digital marketing, social media management and public relations.

It demonstrates how to present the brand by following brand guidelines and how to promote it to generate more business. It provides access to marketing materials, templates and promotional assets for consistent branding across all locations.

- **Day-to-Day Operating Requirements:** This category outlines the daily operational requirements of your franchise such as inventory management, food safety and hygiene, customer service, point-of-sale operations and cash handling. It also includes best practices and troubleshooting guides for various aspects of the business.

- **Development, Growth & Profit:** This category focuses on how to keep finances on track and develop new skills. It provides strategies for growing your franchise, including financial management, performance metrics and key performance indicators (KPIs). It offers guidance on optimising operations, cost control and revenue generation, as well as insights on expansion opportunities such as adding new products, services or locations. It explains how to manage renewal and prepare the business for sale.

Introduction

This precedes the core Categories. The Introduction welcomes the new franchisee to the network, stresses the importance of customer service, quality and teamwork, familiarises potential or new franchisees with the company's history and the marketplace, and describes the franchise 'partnership' and their contribution to the relationship.

It describes the purpose of our Operations Manual, how to use it and the importance of continuous improvement. There's also a comprehensive section on how franchisees must deal ethically with their customers, employees and suppliers, with sustainability at the forefront. Support information encourages the franchisee/manager to immediately contact the right person to seek advice and guidance. There's a handy glossary of 'industry' terms, too. The Introduction has multiple purposes:

- It confirms that the newly signed-up franchisee has made the right choice.

- It explains to a potential franchisee why Patisserie Pénélope should become their franchisor of choice.

- It explains to a potential team member why Patisserie Pénélope should become their employer of choice.

As part of their due diligence, we encourage potential franchisees to read the Introduction to get a feel for our business. However, they must sign an Undertaking of Confidentiality to access more than a simple demonstration of our centralised knowledge-sharing platform and the list of contents for our Core Operating Brand Standards Manual. That way, our IP is protected until they have signed the franchise agreement, are issued with a password and are granted access.

PART TWO

DEVELOPING CONTENT: A BALANCE BETWEEN SWEET AND SAVOURY

Creating great content is like baking a pie. To create a delicious pie, you must balance sweet and savoury flavours and texture for the filling and crust. Similarly, to create great content, you must find the right balance of persuasive language and accurate information to create a satisfying, engaging piece that leaves your audience wanting more.

6
Creating A Knowledge-Sharing Environment

Creating a knowledge-sharing environment (KSE) with the Core Operating Brand Standards Manual (COBSM) at its heart is much like baking a cake. The COBSM is your foundational recipe, ensuring consistency and smooth operation across all the layers of your franchise network.

How you set up your digital COBSM and your KSE depends on whether you are a new, developing, or mature franchisor. In this chapter, I will describe the process of assembling the cake – or creating a KSE – in stages. This allows for better control and efficiency, just like a baker doesn't rush all stages of baking at once.

It is also important to remember that cakes, like franchise networks, need room to grow. Investing in a bigger oven or, in the case of a franchisor, technology and infrastructure, is crucial for scaling up.

By the end of this chapter, you will have learned:

- The options for developing a KSE.

- The importance of scalability and how investing in technology and infrastructure can support the growth of the franchise network.

- How to use your smartphone camera to capture the *Manual Magic* Library QR code to access additional tools and resources.

The three development stages

Stage 1 – Digital version of the COBSM and cloud-based library: Begin by creating a digital version of your COBSM, which comprehensively covers the brand standards, operational guidelines and procedures that all franchisees must adhere to. Then, compile the library of tools and resources that underpins the COBSM. Store these materials in a secure cloud-based storage system, allowing franchisees to access them any time and from any device. Alternatively, you can create a password-protected intranet/franchisee portal on your corporate website, offering a central location for franchisees to access the COBSM, tools and resources.

Stage 2 – Migrate to a formal KMC: As your franchise network grows and the library of tools and resources expands, it's time to migrate to a formal Knowledge Management Centre (KMC). This system should be designed with scalability, allowing for easy expansion as your network grows. Organise and categorise the information within the KMC to ensure easy navigation and retrieval. Incorporate features such as search functionality, user authentication, access control and collaboration tools to facilitate knowledge sharing and streamline communication between franchisees and the franchisor's head office.

Stage 3 – Integration with a knowledge-sharing platform: With a mature network, you could consider adopting a knowledge-sharing platform to further enhance the capabilities of your KMC. A platform like Manual.to[11] offers additional features, such as the ability to create and share step-by-step guides, multimedia support and real-time updates, making it easier for franchisees to access and utilise the information. These platforms also provide advanced analytics and reporting tools, enabling you to monitor usage, identify trends and continuously improve based on user feedback and needs.

---

11   https://manual.to

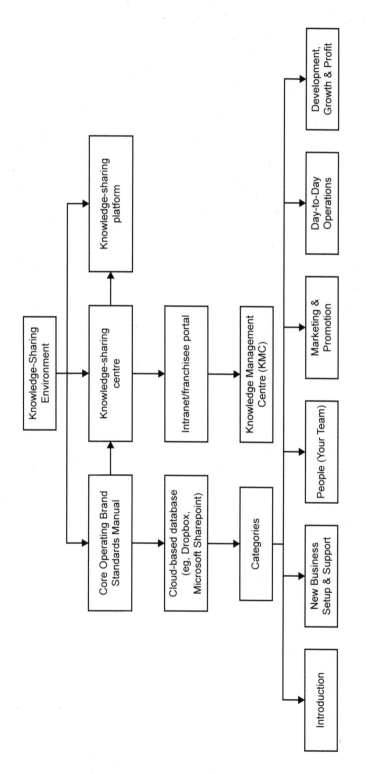

Knowledge-Sharing Environment Options

The diagram represents the journey of a new franchisor creating their first Operations Manual based on a simple knowledge-sharing concept of a COBSM linked to a cloud-based database using the six Categories. As the franchise network matures, it develops into a formal Knowledge Management Centre. With thirty-plus franchisees, it can develop into a full knowledge-sharing platform.

Core Operating Brand Standards Manual

The COBSM underpins the terms and conditions of the franchise agreement and links directly from, and to, your Tools & Resources in your KSE.

The COBSM is a critical component outlining the brand standards, operational guidelines and procedures that all franchisees must adhere to as part of their franchise agreement. The COBSM serves as a foundational reference document, ensuring that your brand identity and quality standards are consistently maintained across all franchise locations.

Using hyperlinks and QR codes: To enhance user experience and efficiency, the COBSM incorporates hyperlinks to the listed Tools & Resources. QR codes and/their URLs can be used for instant access to training materials, marketing assets, financial management templates or Standard Operating Procedures that do not need to be incorporated in the COBSM (eg, brand guidelines, health and safety manual and user guides). Both methods allow franchisees to quickly access the specific tools or resources they need directly from the relevant sections of the COBSM. This results in a lighter version of the traditional text-heavy Operations Manual. Hyperlinks are clearly marked and usually highlighted or underlined with a distinct colour, indicating that they are clickable and will direct the user to the desired information.

Using URLs: Where appropriate, URLs can be placed within the content directing franchisees to external websites – eg, employment and health and safety legislation, data protection guidance and resources, planning applications and permits and approved supplier details. The URLs are clearly marked iterative and usually highlighted or underlined with a colour different from the Tools & Resources hyperlinks, indicating that they are clickable and will direct the user to the desired information.

Mobile and desktop compatibility: The COBSM and its hyperlinks should be designed to be compatible with desktop and mobile devices, ensuring that franchisees can access the necessary tools and resources regardless of the device they are using.

User authentication and access control: The KSE incorporates user authentication and access control mechanisms to ensure that only authorised users can access the COBSM and Tools & Resources. This helps protect the franchisor's proprietary information and maintains the security and confidentiality of the franchise network.

Knowledge-sharing centre

A franchisor can create a knowledge-sharing centre with just one or two franchisees and scale up as the franchise network grows. In fact, starting small can be advantageous as it allows the franchise to develop and refine the knowledge-sharing centre based on the needs and feedback of the initial franchisees. This approach can help ensure that it is tailored to the specific requirements of the franchise and provides maximum value to its users.

A KMC is designed to support the efficient operation and growth of the franchise. It serves as a centralised hub where employees, franchisees and management can access and share the organisation's collective knowledge, expertise and best practices, ensuring a consistent and high-quality experience across all locations. Key components of the Knowledge Management Centre include:

- **Knowledge creation:** For example, the KMC for Patisserie Pénélope would encourage the generation of innovative ideas, recipes and techniques through collaboration between franchise locations, the central kitchen and the franchisor's head office.

- **Knowledge capture:** The system captures both explicit knowledge (eg, Standard Operating Procedures, recipes and training materials) and tacit knowledge (eg, baking tips and customer service techniques) from all stakeholders, including franchisees, employees and suppliers.

- **Knowledge organisation:** The KMC organises information in a structured and logical manner using categories, tags and metadata related to specific Patisserie Pénélope products, processes and locations.

- **Knowledge storage:** A secure, cloud-based repository is used to store and manage the franchise's collective knowledge, ensuring its accessibility and reliability.

- **Knowledge retrieval:** The system allows users to search and retrieve relevant information using keywords, tags, or natural language queries related to all operations.

- **Knowledge sharing and dissemination:** The KMC facilitates communication and collaboration among users through features like discussion forums, chat rooms and social networking tools, fostering a sense of community and shared learning.

- **Knowledge maintenance:** Regular updates, revisions and archival of outdated or obsolete information ensure the KMC remains current and accurate, reflecting the evolving needs of the franchise.

- **User interface and access control:** The KMC features a user-friendly interface with robust access control mechanisms to ensure that only authorised users can access the system and its contents based on their roles within the organisation.

- **Analytics and reporting:** The KMC includes tools to track system usage, identify patterns and generate insights that can help refine and improve operations across the franchise network.

- **Integration with other systems:** The KMC is interoperable with other enterprise software and systems used by the franchisor – eg, point-of-sale, inventory management and team member scheduling – to maximise its effectiveness and utility.

The KMC is designed to cover all essential aspects of the franchise's operation and growth. To achieve this, the KMC is organised into the Categories identified in Chapter 3:

- Introduction
- New Business Setup & Support
- People (Your Team)

- Marketing & Promotion

- Day-to-Day Operating Requirements

- Development, Growth & Profit

By organising the KMC into these sections, the franchisor ensures that franchisees and employees have access to a comprehensive and well-structured knowledge base, empowering them to successfully operate, manage and grow their businesses while maintaining the high standards and values of their brand.

By implementing the KMC, you can harness the collective intelligence of your network, streamline operations and maintain a consistent and high-quality customer experience across all locations. This, in turn, will contribute to the franchise's overall success and reputation in the marketplace.

Scaling up

Here are some steps to create a KMC with a small number of franchisees and scale up over time:

- **Identify key knowledge areas:** Work with the initial franchisees to determine the most critical knowledge areas and resources required for the successful operation of their businesses. This may include training materials, Standard Operating Procedures, marketing materials and financial management tools.

- **Develop an initial version:** Create an initial version of the KMC, focusing on the identified key knowledge areas. This version should be easy to navigate, with a simple interface and clear organisation of information.

- **Obtain feedback:** As the initial franchisees begin to use the KMC, gather feedback on its usability, functionality and content. Encourage franchisees to share their experiences, suggestions and concerns and use this input to refine and improve the KMC.

- **Scale up gradually:** As the franchise network expands, continue to develop and enhance the KMC based on the needs and feedback of the growing user base. This may involve adding new knowledge areas, resources or features, as well as refining existing content to ensure it remains current and relevant.

- **Monitor usage and performance:** Regularly monitor the usage and performance of the KMC to identify trends, patterns and areas for improvement. This can help ensure that the KMC remains an effective tool for knowledge management and continues to meet the evolving needs of the franchise network.

- **Invest in technology and infrastructure:** As the franchise grows, you will need to invest in the technology and infrastructure required to support the KMC's expanding user base. This may include upgrading servers, enhancing data security and improving user authentication and access control mechanisms.

- **Encourage knowledge sharing and collaboration:** Promote a culture of knowledge sharing and collaboration within the franchise network. Encourage franchisees to contribute to the KMC by sharing their experiences, insights and best practices, as well as participating in discussions and collaborative activities.

By starting small and scaling up, you can create a KMC that is tailored to the needs of your franchisees and evolves alongside the growth of the franchise network. This approach can help ensure that the KMC remains a valuable and effective tool for knowledge management and collaboration, contributing to the overall success of the franchise organisation.

Knowledge-sharing platform

There are several advantages to creating a knowledge-sharing platform for your Operations Manual, particularly one that includes multimedia such as video. These include:

- **Improved understanding:** Multimedia can be more engaging and easier to understand than text-based manuals, which can lead to improved understanding and retention of information by franchisees.

- **Consistency:** A knowledge-sharing platform can ensure consistency in training and operations across all franchise locations, which can help to maintain the integrity of the franchise brand.

- **Flexibility:** A knowledge-sharing platform can be accessed from anywhere at any time, providing flexibility for franchisees who may be in remote locations or who have busy schedules.

- **Customisation:** A knowledge-sharing platform can be customised to the specific needs of each franchise location, providing tailored information and training for different franchises.

- **Cost-effective:** Using a knowledge-sharing platform can be more cost-effective than traditional training methods, as it eliminates the need for in-person training sessions and travel expenses.

- **Scalability:** A knowledge-sharing platform can be scaled up or down as needed to accommodate changes in the franchise system or expansion into new markets.

- **Improved feedback:** A knowledge-sharing platform can provide a mechanism for franchisees to give feedback on training and operations, which can help to improve the overall franchise system.

- **Improved productivity:** Using video for workplace instructions can lead to improved productivity as it provides a visual demonstration of how to perform tasks, which can be more efficient than reading instructions.

- **Improved customer satisfaction:** By providing franchisees with a comprehensive and engaging knowledge-sharing platform, they are better equipped to deliver the perfect customer experience, which should lead to improved customer satisfaction and loyalty.

Summary

By acquiring this knowledge and understanding, you will be better equipped to develop a robust and effective KSE that supports the growth and success of your franchise network. With the strong foundation of the Core Operating Brand Standards Manual, underpinned by a library of Tools & Resources and a clear roadmap for scaling up, you will be well-positioned to ensure consistent operations, efficient knowledge sharing and collaboration across all franchise locations.

7
Underpinning The Franchise Agreement

It is fundamental to establish the context for your recipe when starting a baking project, just as it's essential to set the context for each section of your Core Operating Brand Standards Manual (COBSM).

The five standard headings that precede every section of the Structure & Contents serve as your baking recipe. They are clear and precise and provide a reliable guide for what comes next.

These headings allow you to reinforce the terms of the franchise agreement, akin to ensuring every baker understands the specific steps and measurements in a recipe. It's vital that your franchisees, like experienced bakers, read and comprehend these instructions, as it safeguards both parties involved.

By standardising initial headings, you're like a baker ensuring consistency in measuring and mixing ingredients. The result? A more consistent, user-friendly and efficient manual, serving as a universally followed recipe across your franchise network, contributing to its overall success and growth.

Standard Operating Procedures (SOPs) are like the meticulous recipes crafted by skilled bakers. Just as Patisserie Pénélope's recipes provide step-by-step instructions to create exquisite pastries, SOPs guide the franchisee's actions with precision and finesse. They outline the essential ingredients, precise measurements and the exact sequence of actions required to consistently deliver the perfect customer experience.

Like Pénélope's recipes, SOPs embody the art and science of customer service, ensuring that each interaction is infused with the perfect blend of efficiency, quality and attention to detail, resulting in a delectable journey for both customers and employees.

By the end of this chapter, you will:

- Know what these five headings are and why they are essential

- Learn about SOPs

- Use your smartphone camera to capture the *Manual Magic* Library QR code to access an example of Customer Service SOPs & Audit, and a fun team exercise to understand the difference between Operating and Operational.

Five initial headings

These five headings must be added to each of the sections in your Structure & Contents to set the context and enable you to underpin your franchise agreement:

1. Introduction

2. Minimum Operating Standards

3. Roles & Responsibilities

4. Measure, Analyse, Improve

5. Tools & Resources
   (see also Chapter 3, Tools & Resources)

Why standardise headings?

Standardising these five initial headings for each section of your Operations Manual offers many benefits:

- They create a consistent format and structure throughout the manual, making it easier for franchisees to navigate and locate relevant information quickly.

- They ensure that each section covers essential aspects of the topic, providing franchisees with a clear understanding of the requirements, expectations and procedures.

- When franchisees become familiar with the standardised format, they can quickly find and process information, enabling them to perform tasks and make decisions more efficiently.

- They make it simpler for the franchisor to update or revise the manual, ensuring that changes or additions are consistently incorporated across all sections.

- They facilitate better communication between the franchisor and franchisees, as everyone refers to the same structure, reducing misunderstandings or confusion.

- As the franchise network grows and new processes or procedures are introduced, they provide a reliable framework that can be easily expanded and adapted.

- They help ensure that all franchisees comply with the same minimum operating standards and roles and responsibilities, leading to better compliance and quality control across the franchise network.

- They simplify training and onboarding for new franchisees, who can quickly grasp the structure of the manual and understand the expectations for each section.

A well-structured and consistently formatted manual reflects a high level of professionalism and attention to detail, instilling confidence in franchisees that they are part of a well-organised and reliable franchise model and Business System. Standard headings also facilitate easier benchmarking and performance tracking, as each section provides a clear framework for measuring, analysing and improving operations.

1. Introduction

Crafting the Introduction to a section of your Operations Manual is essential for setting the context and engaging your audience. In the Patisserie Pénélope case study I emphasised the importance of attracting and recruiting the best talent. Let's say we want to develop the first section for 'Recruiting the Best People' under People (Your Team).

Begin by stating the purpose of the section, which is to ensure that all franchisees recruit the best team members.

- Emphasise the importance of recruiting the right people for the success of the franchise against the roles defined in the franchise structure. Explain how it contributes to employee retention, customer satisfaction and overall business growth.

- Tell the franchisee what they can expect to learn from this section, including key principles, best practices and actionable strategies for recruiting top talent.

- Highlight available resources, tools and support offered by the franchisor to assist in the recruitment process – eg, access to job-posting templates, interview guides or assistance from HR specialists.

- Invite franchisees to contact (head office/ franchise manager) for advice, guidance and support. Encourage them to provide feedback on the effectiveness of the provided guidelines, as well as any suggestions for improvement or additional resources they may need.

- Give a bullet point overview of the key topics that the reader will know, understand or learn after reading the section – eg, job-posting creation, candidate sourcing, interview techniques and making recruitment decisions.

Write the Introduction in a clear, concise and engaging tone to make it accessible and easy for franchisees to understand. Carefully proofread and revise it to ensure that it's free of errors and effectively communicates your intended message.

EXAMPLE: 1.0 Introduction

All applicants, whether successful or not, will judge you by the quality of the experience they receive. They may be customers or potential customers and have the power to recommend your [store] to their family, friends and colleagues. We must ensure that all forms of contact with Patisserie Pénélope are positive and that it leaves a good impression of how we value our staff.

The costs associated with recruiting, inducting and training new staff are substantial, so it is in the interests of the franchisee and every store owner/manager to recruit the best staff, with the correct balance of skills, knowledge and behaviours.

Staff must always be recruited with a view to long-term employment because maintaining a stable team is beneficial to staff morale, the smooth running of the store and the delivery of consistent customer service.

We recommend that transparent structures support retention as they enable staff at all levels to see a career progression path. This will motivate individuals and inspire them to commit to further training and development for future roles.

To uphold our reputation in the local marketplace – and globally – you must follow our recruitment process.

By the end of this section, you will:

- Understand how to deliver a professional and consistent recruitment process for your store, in compliance with employment laws
- Know how to identify the role that you need and the person you are seeking

- Know how to attract the right people to a vacancy
- Know how to check applications and select the right candidates for an interview
- Learn how to interview candidates
- Know how to make an offer to, or reject, a candidate

---

2. Minimum Operating Standards

Creating Minimum Operating Standards is crucial to maintain consistency and quality across all franchise locations. Familiarise yourself with the franchise agreement and any related documents to ensure that the standards you develop are aligned with the overall goals, values and requirements of the franchise. Continuing with our section example:

- Break down the recruitment process into key areas, such as job postings, candidate sourcing, application review, interview process, selection criteria and onboarding.

- For each key recruitment area, create a set of minimum standards that franchisees must meet. These should reflect your values, industry best practices and legal requirements.

All job postings must include a clear job title, an accurate description of duties, required qualifications and a statement about the franchisor's commitment to equal-opportunity employment.

Franchisees must utilise a minimum of two different channels to source candidates, such as online job boards, social media or local job fairs – or leading-edge recruitment software such as eTalent Recruitment Software.

- Outline a clear selection process, including any mandatory steps, such as background checks, reference checks or skills assessments.

- Clearly state the mandatory training and onboarding programmes for new team members, including any franchise-specific training modules or certifications.

- Establish specific timeframes for each step of the recruitment process, such as a maximum number of days between receiving an application and scheduling an interview or making a hiring decision.

- Specify any reporting requirements related to recruitment, such as the submission of employment reports or documentation of compliance with equal opportunity laws.

- Provide franchisees with access to tools and resources such as templates and guides and resources to help them meet the established minimum operating standards, such as job posting templates, interview guides or onboarding checklists.

- Define your process for monitoring and evaluating compliance with the minimum operating standards and outline the consequences for non-compliance.

Regularly review and update the minimum operating standards to reflect any changes in the company's values, industry best practices or legal requirements. Write the standards in a clear and concise tone to ensure they are easily understood and followed by franchisees. Finally, carefully proofread and revise the document to ensure it's free of errors and effectively communicates the desired standards.

EXAMPLE: 1.1 Minimum operating standards

Prior to market opening, all franchisees must ensure that:

- Recruitment procedures comply with current employment legislation, the franchise agreement and any other legal or regulatory requirements.
- Dedicated individuals are appointed to team roles as specified in the Patisserie Pénélope business management and team member structures.
- The key personnel identified in the business management structure are sourced and recruited against Patisserie Pénélope job descriptions and candidate profiles in accordance with our requirements.
- Candidates are recruited with the appropriate character traits, behaviours and attributes who have

(or can develop) the skills necessary for delivering customer and operational excellence within their roles.

- Team members know what is expected of them and are confident in the delivery of their roles.

- Sufficient staff are recruited for each (store) to deliver service that meets the franchisor's core values.

- All applicants are aware of the career progression opportunities available through the franchisor's training programme.

- Proof is obtained for all members of staff who are eligible to work in the UK.

- Suitable onboarding is conducted for all new employees.

- All key personnel attend and meet the appropriate requirements for brand induction and initial training.

- Staff turnover is minimised to maintain stable teams and deliver superior customer service – the Patisserie Pénélope way – consistently to every customer.

- Every new member of staff is issued with a contract of employment before taking up their appointment.

- All completed selection tools – including application forms and CVs – are kept for a minimum of twelve months or in accordance with current government guidance.

Employment law is complex and constantly evolving, so many franchisors use or recommend third-party HR support for the creation of employee contracts and to support the ongoing management of franchise teams.

3. Roles & Responsibilities

Creating a comprehensive Roles & Responsibilities heading is essential for defining the expectations of all involved parties.

Determine the key stakeholders involved in the recruitment process, including franchisees, managers, HR personnel and any support staff from the franchisor's head office.

Clearly outline the roles and titles of each stakeholder involved in the recruitment process. For each role, list their specific responsibilities in the recruitment process. Use bullet points or numbered lists to make the information easy to read and understand.

Explain the hierarchy and decision-making process for each stage of recruitment, such as who has the final say on hiring decisions and any necessary approvals from the franchisor.

Outline the preferred communication channels and protocols between stakeholders, such as regular meetings, reporting requirements, or the use of specific software or tools.

- Provide access to templates, guidelines, and resources that support stakeholders in fulfilling their roles and responsibilities, such as job posting templates, interview guides, and onboarding checklists. Use hyperlinks to access them from your library of Tools & Resources.

- Highlight the importance of collaboration and teamwork among all stakeholders to ensure a smooth and efficient recruitment process that aligns with the franchise's values and goals.

- Identify common challenges or obstacles that may arise during the recruitment process and provide guidance on how to overcome them, such as handling difficult interviews or managing a high volume of applications.

- Invite franchisees to provide feedback on their experiences with the recruitment process, as well as suggestions for improvement or additional resources they may need.

Write the Roles & Responsibilities section using clear, concise language that is easy for all stakeholders to understand. Carefully proofread and revise the section to ensure it is free of errors and effectively communicates the roles and responsibilities of all stakeholders in the recruitment process.

EXAMPLE: 1.2 Roles & Responsibilities

- Franchisor: Provides guidance, resources and training materials to assist franchisees in the recruitment process.
- Franchisee/Manager: Oversees the entire recruitment process, approves final employment

decisions, monitors to ensure compliance with legal and franchise requirements and maintains personnel records. Delivers brand and induction training.

- Assistant Manager: Develops job descriptions, assists with postings, screens applications, conducts interviews and coordinates onboarding and training for new team members.

---

4. Measure, Analyse, Improve

Creating a 'Measure, Analyse, Improve' heading is crucial for continuously optimising the recruitment process and ensuring consistent performance across the franchise network:

- State the purpose, which is to guide franchisees in measuring, analysing and improving their recruitment processes to consistently recruit the best people.

- Identify the KPIs relevant to the recruitment process such as time to employ, cost per employee, candidate satisfaction, employee retention and quality of employee.

- Outline the methods for collecting data on each KPI, such as conducting surveys, tracking software or using management reports.

- Establish benchmarks and targets for each KPI, which may be based on industry standards, company-wide goals or the performance of top-performing franchisees.

- Explain how to analyse the collected data to identify trends, areas of strength and areas for improvement. This may include comparing actual performance against targets, identifying patterns or analysing the impact of specific recruitment strategies.

- Offer actionable strategies and best practices for improving performance in each area such as refining job postings, enhancing interview techniques or investing in additional training and development. Add any cross-references to the Development, Growth & Profit section using a hyperlink.

- Emphasise the importance of continuously monitoring and evaluating recruitment performance to ensure long-term success and adaptability to changing circumstances.

- Encourage franchisees to collaborate and share their best practices and lessons learned with one another, fostering a culture of continuous improvement across the network.

- Highlight any available resources, tools or support provided by the franchisor to assist franchisees in their efforts to measure, analyse and improve their recruitment processes such as access to data analytics software or consultations with HR specialists.

- Suggest a schedule for conducting regular reviews and updates to the recruitment process, such as quarterly or annual assessments, to ensure ongoing effectiveness and alignment with the franchise's values and goals.

Write the Measure, Analyse, Improve section using clear, concise language that is easy for franchisees to understand and follow. Carefully proofread and revise the section to ensure it is free of errors and effectively communicates the desired guidance for optimising recruitment practices.

Regular reviews of every aspect of your franchisee's recruitment process will enable them to identify and focus on procedural excellence and help them identify any areas that can be improved within the business. Measuring, analysing and improving recruitment processes involves several key steps.

EXAMPLE: 1.3 Measure, Analyse, Improve

1.3.1 Identify objectives

Clearly define the goals of the recruitment process, such as attracting a diverse pool of qualified candidates, reducing 'time to fill' and improving retention rates. Identify and establish measurable KPIs that align with the recruitment objectives. Common KPIs include:

- 'Time to fill'
- Cost per employee
- Quality of employee

- Candidate experience
- Source of recruitment
- Diversity and inclusion metrics
- Offer acceptance rate
- Employee referral rate
- Turnover/retention

1.3.2 Collect data

Set up systems to collect data throughout the recruitment process. This may include applicant tracking systems (ATS), HR software and spreadsheets.

1.3.3 Analyse the data

Analyse the recruitment KPIs and reports to identify trends, bottlenecks and areas for improvement. Compare the results with industry benchmarks and the franchise's past performance.

1.3.4 Identify areas for improvement

Based on the analysis, pinpoint specific areas where improvements can be made. For example, if 'time to fill' is higher than the industry average, focusing on refining job descriptions, sourcing strategies and streamlining interviews may help.

1.3.5 Implement changes and track progress

Make the necessary changes in the recruitment process and continue to monitor the KPIs to assess the effectiveness of the interventions.

1.3.6 Review and adapt

As specified, review the process and update KPIs, goals and objectives based on the ongoing results and feedback. Continuously improve the recruitment process by incorporating feedback from candidates and recruitment managers, and adapting to the changing talent landscape.

1.3.7 Train and involve stakeholders

Ensure that everyone involved in the recruitment process is trained and informed about the objectives, KPIs, and improvement initiatives. Encourage collaboration and communication among recruiters, recruitment managers, HR and other stakeholders to align their efforts.

1.3.8 Use technology to optimise processes

Utilise HR tech tools and analytics platforms to automate tasks and enhance the recruitment process. This can include using AI for candidate screening, chatbots for candidate engagement, video interviewing tools and more.

1.3.9 Foster a strong employer brand

A compelling employer brand is invaluable in attracting and retaining top talent. Regularly assess and develop the franchisor's brand standard to become 'the employer of choice' by promoting a positive corporate culture, highlighting team member success stories and showcasing the company's values and achievements in the job market.

---

5. Tools & Resources

A franchise manager needs a variety of tools and resources to effectively advertise for, select and recruit new team members. Here are some key tools that can be listed for this process.

EXAMPLE: 1.4 Tools & Resources

- **Job roles:** Clearly defined job roles outline the specific responsibilities, tasks and expectations for each position within the organisation. This helps candidates understand the requirements and assess their suitability for the role.

- **Job descriptions:** Comprehensive job descriptions detail the qualifications, experience and skills needed for a specific role, as well as any specific traits or abilities that are desirable for a successful candidate.

- **Recruitment channels:** Franchise managers need to select appropriate recruitment channels such as job boards, social media or industry-specific websites to advertise job openings and reach their target candidate pool.

- **Applicant tracking system (ATS):** An ATS helps manage the recruitment process by organising and tracking job applications, filtering candidates based on predefined criteria and streamlining communication with applicants.

- **Interview templates:** Structured interview templates with predetermined questions and evaluation criteria can help ensure a consistent and unbiased assessment of a candidate's skills, experience and fit for the role.

- **Behavioural and technical assessments:** Standardised assessments can be used to evaluate candidates' technical skills, problem-solving abilities or behavioural traits relevant to the job role. For example, psychometric assessments cover intelligence, aptitudes and skills and personality.

- **Reference check templates:** Templates for conducting reference checks help ensure that relevant information about a candidate's past performance, work ethic and interpersonal skills is gathered from previous employers or colleagues.
- **Employment contracts:** Standardised employment contracts outline the terms and conditions of employment, including job responsibilities, salary, benefits, working hours and termination procedures.
- **Onboarding checklists:** A well-structured onboarding checklist helps ensure that new team members receive necessary training, support and resources to perform their job effectively and integrate into the organisation.
- **Employee handbooks:** These documents provide information on company policies, procedures and expectations, as well as any relevant industry-specific regulations or guidelines.

Creating Standard Operating Procedures

An SOP is a detailed set of instructions that guide the expected routine tasks and activities in a franchise. They provide a framework for continuous improvement in your franchise. Creating a set of SOPs for your franchise is essential. They play an instrumental role in ensuring operational efficiency, maintaining quality standards and promoting safety. SOPs are meant to be followed exactly as written each and every time the task is performed to maintain consistency, efficiency and quality:

- **Consistency:** SOPs ensure that every franchisee operates in the same manner, leading to consistent product quality and customer experience across different locations. This is vital for maintaining your brand's reputation and customer loyalty.

- **Efficiency:** SOPs provide clear guidance on how tasks must be performed, reducing the need for decision-making and trial and error, and leading to increased productivity and efficiency.

- **Training:** SOPs serve as an excellent training resource for new employees, helping them understand their roles and responsibilities quickly and accurately. They also provide a reference for employees to refresh their understanding of tasks.

- **Compliance:** SOPs help ensure that your franchises comply with industry regulations and safety standards, thereby minimising the risk of violations and accidents.

- **Quality control:** By standardising procedures, you ensure a consistent level of quality in your products and services, which is crucial for customer satisfaction.

- **Business continuity:** In case of employee absence or equipment failure, SOPs ensure that the business can continue running smoothly without disruption. New employees can follow the SOPs to quickly get up to speed.

- **Performance measurement and improvement:** SOPs provide a benchmark for performance. They can be reviewed and updated as necessary for continuous improvement based on feedback and changing business needs.

Use your smartphone to capture the *Manual Magic* Library QR code and access an example of Customer Service SOPs & Audit.

manualmagic.manual.to/library

Many procedures can be captured quickly and efficiently using a smartphone. See Chapter 8, Considering A Richer, More Engaging Experience and the example in our fictional franchise Patisserie Pénélope in Chapter 5.

Operating vs operational?

We often hear people asking for what they want, such as 'good', 'the right size', 'on time', 'regularly', or 'frequently'. These words mean something to the person using them. They also mean something to the person hearing them. But will the two meanings be the same? Only the use of operational definitions can guarantee a correct interpretation.

A definition explains what something means. An operational definition does much more. It describes how something should be observed, measured or decided. Without explanations, ambiguity can quickly arise. The training seeks to qualify operational definitions and demonstrate that only the highest quality service and product standards are acceptable. When initial training has been completed, the Operations Manual becomes every franchisee's term of reference.

However, operational definitions are required to sufficiently describe all the steps necessary to complete a given task to the required quality standards. An operational process is an organised set of activities or tasks that leads to excellence for a specific service or product. Usually, it addresses what, when, why, who and how questions.

For example, in a food service franchise, the easy option would be to tell the franchisees that cleaning must be done frequently. But this means nothing. The franchisor must explain:

- What must be cleaned (kitchen floor, equipment, countertop surfaces, etc).

- Why this is essential.

- Who is responsible for ensuring cleanliness to the franchisor's minimum operating standard.

- What utensils and approved cleaning solutions must be used.

- What the logical steps are when carrying out the work.

- How often cleaning must take place, and at what times.

Operating checklists are convenient as aides-mémoires – eg, a store standards checklist to be used by the franchisee/manager to ensure that specified jobs are completed.

How to write an SOP

When explaining to a content expert how to write a SOP, it is important to emphasise clarity, structure and accuracy.

Note: In all procedures that are mandatory the language used is must – ie, 'You must comply with the franchise agreement and all regulatory requirements.'

Although best practice is often thought of as discretionary, the implication is that it must be followed. An example is: 'We strongly recommend you follow this [best practice].'

Here's a step-by-step guide to help you and your team members write an effective operational procedure:

1. **Understand the process:** Begin by gaining a thorough understanding of the process for which the operational procedure is being written. This may involve talking to subject matter experts, observing the process in action or reviewing existing documentation.

2. **Define the objective:** Clearly state the objective of the procedure, specifying the desired outcome and any key goals or targets. This will help guide the overall structure and content of the procedure.

3. **Identify the target audience:** Determine who must follow the operational procedure, such as the franchise manager, designated team member or external contractor. This will influence the level of detail and complexity required in the documentation.

4. **Break down the process:** Break the process down into a series of sequential steps, ensuring each step is clear, concise and easy to understand. Use simple language and avoid jargon or technical terms wherever possible.

5. **Use clear formatting:** Format the operational procedure using numbered or bulleted lists, headings and subheadings to make it easy for readers to follow. Consistent formatting will help users quickly locate relevant information.

6. **Include visual aids:** Use the 'how-to' video as described in my Patisserie Pénélope case study, diagrams, flowcharts or images to illustrate complex concepts or steps, making the procedure more accessible and engaging for the target audience.

7. **Detail roles and responsibilities:** Specify the roles and responsibilities of individuals involved in each step of the process, including any required approvals, collaboration or communication.

8. **Address potential challenges:** Identify any common challenges or obstacles that may arise during the process and provide guidance on how to overcome or mitigate them.

9. **Reference related documents:** Include references to any related documents, forms or resources that users may need to complete the procedure, such as templates, checklists or policy documents.

10. **Establish a review process:** Implement a process for regularly reviewing and updating the operational procedure to ensure it remains accurate, relevant and effective over time.

11. **Test and refine:** Before finalising the operational procedure, have individuals from the target audience test the document to ensure it is clear, accurate and easy to follow. Gather feedback and make any necessary revisions to improve the document's clarity and effectiveness.

12. **Proofread and edit:** Carefully proofread and edit the operational procedure to ensure it's free of errors, inconsistencies or ambiguities. This will help ensure the document is professional and easy to understand.

By following these steps, the content expert can create an operational procedure that is clear, effective and easy for users to follow, ultimately improving process efficiency and consistency.

Summary

- Five headings set the context for the Standard Operating Procedures (SOPs) that follow.

- SOPs play an instrumental role in ensuring operational efficiency, maintaining quality standards, promoting safety and providing a framework for continuous improvement.

- SOPs are meant to be followed exactly as written, each and every time the task is performed, to maintain consistency, efficiency and quality.

8
Considering Multimedia Tools

Baking a cake is an art that involves more than just mixing ingredients together. It's about layering flavours, textures and colours to create a masterpiece that delights the senses. Similarly, an Operations Manual utilising multimedia tools is like adding different ingredients to the recipe for success.

Think of video as the sweet and indulgent frosting that can take your franchise to new heights. Just as there are endless possibilities when it comes to incorporating video in baking, its applications in a franchise are vast and powerful. It's not limited to social media marketing; video can be a potent tool for communication, daily operations and business growth.

Just as a beautifully decorated cake captures attention, video training captures the hearts and minds of franchisees and their teams. It taps into the power of visual learning and offers flexibility, consistency, efficiency and increased engagement. It's like a step-by-step tutorial that guides franchisees through the process, ensuring they understand and retain the necessary knowledge.

Creating video content is akin to crafting the perfect slice of cake for your knowledge-sharing resource or formal knowledge-sharing platform. The approach and execution may differ based on the environment you create. If you opt for a knowledge-sharing resource, your video creation approach will have its unique characteristics. On the other hand, if you utilise a knowledge-sharing platform, your video strategy will take a different shape with its own set of benefits.

By the end of this chapter, you will:

- Understand the power of using video to train your teams

- Learn why it's a vital element for knowledge sharing

- Know what additional multimedia tools are available

- Use your smartphone camera to capture the *Manual Magic* Resource Centre QR code to access additional Tools & Resources

Training

Training videos can cover topics such as:

- Product and service offers

- Customer service

- Marketing and sales

- Safety and compliance

- Training reinforcement

Video is a highly effective way to train franchisees and their staff on various aspects of the business for several reasons:

1. Visual learning: As humans, we are naturally more visually oriented, and our brains are wired to process visual information more quickly and effectively than text or oral communication. Videos use visual and auditory senses to present information more engagingly and memorably. Many learners learn best by seeing things. Video provides a rich, dynamic visual experience that allows learners to see and understand the material in a way that text-based materials cannot match.

2. Demonstrations: Videos can show actual demonstrations of the tasks or procedures, allowing the learners to see the steps and techniques involved. This can be especially valuable for franchises that involve complex processes or equipment, such as food preparation or machinery operation.

3. Consistency: Video training ensures that every employee sees and hears the same information presented in the same way. This helps to ensure consistency in how the franchise is run and can reduce the risk of errors or misunderstandings.

4. Flexibility: Video training can be accessed any time and anywhere, and can be paused, rewound and replayed. This allows employees to learn at their own pace and review material as often as necessary.

5. Efficiency: Video training can be completed in less time than traditional classroom or paper-based training. It eliminates the need for travel to attend training sessions and allows employees to complete training independently without disrupting the regular work schedule.

6. Engagement: Video is a highly engaging medium that can help to hold learners' attention and increase their motivation to learn. This can lead to better information retention and improved job performance.

Currently, it's the closest we can come to on-the-job training with an excellent trainer. But, of course, not all teachers will deliver the same excellent learning experience across a franchise network. This leads to inconsistency: there's no single source of truth with different teachers. Video can offer a single source of truth, improving standardisation.

Franchisees can access the videos any time and anywhere. They can also review the content as many times as needed. You can even create interactive videos and quizzes to underline learning and confirm compliance.

Marketing

Video marketing helps franchisees attract customers, increase brand awareness and differentiate themselves from competitors. These are examples of how video creates compelling promotional content for a franchise:

1. Product or service demos: Videos showcase the franchise's products or services in action, highlighting their features, benefits and unique value propositions.

2. Customer testimonials: Videos feature satisfied customers sharing their positive experiences with the franchise's products or services. This helps build trust and credibility.

3. Brand storytelling: Videos tell the story of the franchise, its history, values, mission and culture. They help to create an emotional connection with the target audience. This is particularly powerful if the franchisor or franchisee shares their story and vision personally.

4. Social media content: Videos help increase the franchise's social media following and drive sales. They create engaging content for platforms in accordance with the franchisor's guidelines. Short, engaging videos generate buzz and attract followers on social media platforms like Facebook, LinkedIn, Instagram, YouTube, TikTok and, possibly, Snapchat. For example, franchisees can post videos of their daily routines, behind-the-scenes footage or funny outtakes to entertain and engage their audience.

Communication

Video facilitates communication between the franchisor and franchisees. This includes videos from the franchisor providing franchisees with updates, guidance or feedback. These are examples of communication videos:

- **Corporate updates:** Videos from the franchisor provide franchisees with the latest news, announcements and changes to the business. These videos are more engaging and informative than emails or newsletters.

- **A podcast:** A visual internal 'podcast' is a great way to keep the network informed, provide additional value to franchisees, and engage them by appearing as guests to share their stories and successes.

- **Training feedback:** Videos provide feedback on franchisees' training progress and performance. This helps identify areas for improvement and ensure consistency in the brand experience.

- **Best practices sharing:** Videos can showcase successful franchisees or team members sharing their best practices and tips for success. This inspires and motivates others to improve their performance.

Video communication builds trust, transparency and accountability between franchisors and franchisees.

Operations

Video is used to improve operational efficiency and quality control. For example, video is used to monitor and improve the quality of food preparation or the cleanliness of facilities. These are examples of operational videos:

- **Quality control checks:** Videos can monitor and audit the quality of services or products delivered by franchisees. This helps ensure consistency and compliance with the franchisor's standards.

- **Maintenance and repair:** Videos can provide a guide on how to maintain and repair equipment, facilities or vehicles that franchisees use. This helps reduce downtime and repair costs.

Video operations help improve productivity, reduce errors and enhance customer satisfaction.

Franchise development

Video is used to attract potential franchisees to the business. This includes videos showcasing the franchise's success stories and the benefits of owning a franchise. These are examples of franchise development videos:

- **Franchisee success stories:** Videos can showcase successful franchisees sharing their stories of how they started and grew their businesses. These videos are powerful testimonials for the franchise's potential profitability and growth opportunities.

- **Virtual tours:** Videos can provide virtual tours of the franchise's facilities, equipment and operations. This helps potential franchisees better understand the Business System and processes.

- **Q&A sessions:** Videos can feature the franchisor and existing franchisees answering questions from potential franchisees. This helps clarify doubts and provides more information about the franchise opportunity.

- **Personalised videos:** Using videos during the sales funnel can be a great way of engaging potential franchisees and encouraging them to accept a discovery call.

Franchise development videos help the franchisor attract qualified and motivated franchisees, expand the franchise network and achieve growth goals.

Performing tasks

Using video to demonstrate how to perform a task is very effective because it allows the viewer to see exactly how it's done. This can be especially useful for tasks that involve multiple steps or are difficult to explain in writing.

When we 'show' something in a video, we use images, sounds and movement to convey information rather than relying solely on verbal descriptions. This can create a more engaging and immersive experience for the franchise team member, as they can see and hear the story unfold in real time.

Captions

Even when using visual storytelling techniques, providing some context or additional information can still help the viewer understand what is happening. This is where captions come in:

- Using video with captions effectively demonstrates visual storytelling's 'show, don't tell' principle.

- Captions provide a written description of the video's action, dialogue and other important information. It helps to clarify any details that might otherwise be unclear. This can be especially helpful for viewers who are deaf or hard of hearing and those who may be watching in a noisy environment or without sound.

- Captions and video transcripts are especially helpful for those for whom English is a second language.

In short, using video with captions allows us to 'show' the story through visual and auditory elements while providing the necessary information through written text. This can create a more engaging and accessible experience for franchisees. It helps to reinforce the principle of 'show, don't tell' in visual storytelling.

The evidence

Evidence supports the claim that video allows for a more immersive and engaging learning experience. Several studies have demonstrated the benefits of video over text in workplace training.

The study, 'Learning by watching others learn: the use of videoed tutorials in undergraduate business education', investigates how much student observers learn from watching or observing videoed tutorials.[12] Encouragingly, watching videos of tutorial dialogues has, in some situations, been found to be as effective as being physically present in a tutorial and results in higher levels of engagement and motivation among learners.

Kevin Aires, founder and managing director of Cadenz Video Academy, coaches franchisors and franchisees on creating the video content they need for their 'Know Like Trust' customer journey. He coaches clients to create their own Know Like Trust content or uses remote capture to do it for them to accelerate their journey. He says,

> 'We know that people buy from people, but now, 70% of the customer journey happens before people meet you, so how can you meet them... before you meet them. The answer is obvious: video.

> 'The emotional, decision-making part of the brain can't tell the difference between video and meeting someone face to face. Video of you multiplies you and can be out there selling and communicating for you day and night, educating and informing your audience 24-7.

---

12 S Geertshuis et al, 'Learning by watching others learn: the use of videoed tutorials in undergraduate business education', *Higher Education Pedagogies*, Volume 6, Issue 1 (2021), www.tandfonline. com/doi/full/10.1080/23752696.2021.1916980, accessed 18 July 2023

At the same time, *text* about you can only really inform.

'Video of you sharing the same information allows your audience to like and trust you and move along that 70% of the customer journey to where they can meet the real you. If you're not intentionally creating that engaging journey – largely using video – guess what: someone else is.'

Hints and tips

Before filming, planning out the shots you want to capture is essential. This will help you complete all critical steps and ensure you have everything you need to create clear and comprehensive work instructions.

- Create a shot list with a still for the title, close-ups, medium shots and wide shots that best demonstrate each procedure step.

- Consider using storyboarding to help visualise your shots.

Other multimedia tools

Additional multimedia tools can be included in your Operations Manual KSE. They can provide a rich and engaging learning experience for franchisees and their teams because they cater to different learning styles and preferences. See Chapter 9 for how video is used on a knowledge-sharing platform.

They can also make the learning process more effective and enjoyable, but you must be mindful of costs, consistency and complexity. Sometimes a plain and simple knowledge repository such as Manual.to would be beneficial because it provides a simple, standardised interface that people feel confident in using. Examples of multimedia tools include:

- **Audio recordings:** Audio recordings of lectures, interviews and podcasts can be listened to on the go or while doing other activities.

- **Animations:** Animations are dynamic visual aids that can help us to understand complex concepts by breaking them down into simple, step-by-step processes. However, these can be expensive and usually only afforded by large, mature franchises.

- **Infographics:** Infographics are visual representations of information that help to make complex data or concepts more easily understandable by presenting them in a visual and easily digestible format.

- **Interactive media:** Interactive media such as quizzes, games and simulations can help engage learners and reinforce concepts by providing hands-on learning and practice opportunities.

However, these are only worth the investment if you have a substantial franchisee network.

- **Virtual Reality (VR) and Augmented Reality (AR):** VR and AR technologies are immersive and interactive, providing learners with a realistic and engaging learning experience that can help to reinforce concepts and procedures. Again, the investment can only be justified if you are a substantial franchise.

- **Webinars and live streaming:** Webinars and live streaming sessions provide a live and interactive learning experience that allows learners to ask questions and interact with instructors and other learners in real-time.

In the age of YouTube, Instagram and TikTok, it is essential for franchisors to adapt their strategies to align with the changing preferences of their target audience. They must embrace the shift towards a younger workforce with shorter attention spans.

Summary

- Creating video content should be considered a vital element of a franchisor's knowledge-sharing resource.

- Video communication builds trust, transparency and accountability between franchisor and franchisees.

- Franchisee team members can benefit from visual rather than text-based instructions, particularly those involving complex processes, equipment or procedures.

- Multimedia tools can be used to provide a rich and engaging learning experience.

- How you record workplace instructions on video will vary according to whether you add it to a knowledge-sharing centre or a formal platform such as Manual.to.

9
Considering A Richer, More Engaging Experience

In the world of baking, every good recipe starts with a solid foundation of essential ingredients. From there, it's up to the baker to infuse creativity and innovation to make a mouth-watering cake that stands out from the rest. Similarly, in the realm of creating an Operations Manual, it's crucial to recognise the changing landscape of information consumption and adapt accordingly.

Just as people's tastes and preferences have evolved in the baking world, the YouTube, Instagram and Tik-Tok era has revolutionised how individuals seek and absorb information. Attention spans have become shorter, and there is a growing demand for content that is quick and easy to digest. This shift is particularly pronounced among younger generations who crave instant solutions to their information needs and rely on trusted peers for guidance rather than solely relying on corporate information.

Imagine your franchise Operations Manual as a scrumptious cake. The traditional approach may have served its purpose, so it's time to take your recipe to the next level. In this chapter, we will explore how you can provide your franchisees with a richer, more engaging experience that leaves a lasting impression, just like a cake that tantalises tastebuds and leaves everyone wanting more.

We will delve into the reasons why a richer, more engaging experience is essential for your franchisees. You will discover how simple it is to infuse creativity into your workplace instructions by leveraging knowledge sharing that caters to modern consumption patterns. Furthermore, we will unlock the value of QR codes, which can act as secret ingredients that add an extra layer of convenience and accessibility to your Operations Manual.

So, grab your metaphorical apron and let's embark on this baking journey together. By the time we're finished, you'll have the knowledge and tools to create engaging content that not only satisfies the hunger for information, but also leaves your franchisees eager to become involved.

By the end of this chapter, you will:

- Learn why you should provide your franchisees with a richer, more engaging experience

- Learn how simple it is to create more engaging workplace instructions for knowledge sharing

- Understand the value of QR codes

- Use your smartphone camera to capture the *Manual Magic* Library QR code to access fifty workplace instructions for Patisserie Pénélope in a 'show don't tell' format that could be demonstrated in a 'how-to' video

Peer-to-peer engagement

Nowadays, people are more likely to engage with content from their peers than traditional, corporate sources. This preference can be attributed to several factors, including relatability, authenticity and trust. Research conducted by the Edelman Trust Barometer[13] reveals that trust in businesses has decreased, while trust in peers has increased. This highlights the importance of peer-to-peer engagement in the current digital landscape. For younger generations, including

---

13   Edelman, 'Special Report: The New Cascade Of Influence' (Edelman, 2022), www.edelman.com/sites/g/files/aatuss191/ files/2022-06/Top%2010%20-%202022%20Edelman%20Trust%20 Barometer%20Special%20Report-%20The%20New%20Cascade%20 of%20Influence.pdf

Millennials and Gen Z, this effect is amplified through their different use of technology, with a strong focus on short-form video.

By creating content that caters to shorter attention spans and prioritising peer-to-peer engagement, franchises can better attract and retain these younger generations.

Implications for franchising

These consumption pattern changes have significant implications for franchising – and the traditional text-heavy Operations Manual. To remain competitive and relevant, franchisors need to embrace peer-to-peer learning. They must adapt their communication and training strategies to meet the demands of franchisees' new team members.

Providing information in concise, visually appealing formats such as videos and infographics is more likely to resonate with franchisees' team members. Furthermore, leveraging user-generated content and testimonials from existing franchisees can help build trust and credibility. For example, a franchisor could create a series of short, engaging videos addressing common questions and challenges faced by franchisees. These videos could be shared on social media platforms, where potential franchisees are more likely to encounter and engage with them.

Standard Operating Procedures (SOPs)

The shift in information consumption patterns has implications for SOPs in franchising. SOPs, critical for ensuring consistency and quality across a franchise, must be accessible and easy to understand. Traditional text-heavy manuals may no longer be the most effective method for communicating this information.

To cater to the preferences of the younger generation, SOPs should be adapted to incorporate more visual elements such as videos, images and flowcharts. These formats can help convey complex information more digestibly, improving comprehension and retention. Additionally, incorporating interactive elements such as quizzes or simulations can help franchisees engage with the material more effectively.

It's also important to consider the role of peer-to-peer engagement in the context of SOPs. Creating opportunities for franchisees to share their experiences, best practices and insights can foster a sense of community and trust, ultimately contributing to the success of the entire franchise network.

Knowledge-sharing platform

In Patisserie Pénélope, our fictional case study, video is the key to swiftly and efficiently creating their Operations Manual on a knowledge-sharing platform such as Manual.to. It is also fundamental for sharing knowledge and obtaining greater engagement with the franchisee's team members. Jorim Rademaker, founder and CEO of Manual.to, explains:

> 'The workforce is changing. A new generation is emerging. The employee that you thought you needed doesn't exist anymore. So, it's not a contest to attract the best talent, because that person doesn't exist. Demographics are changing. Increasingly, the talent pool will consist of people with diverse backgrounds without the necessary skills or qualifications.'

There's a scene in *The Matrix* where Neo plugs a cable into his mind and suddenly, he knows kung fu! Instant knowledge in a dream world. Of course, that doesn't happen in reality, but how close can we get to that point? 'Today, the fastest way to get as close as possible to this is on-the-job learning with an experienced mentor,' Jorim comments.

> 'The single most efficient way to learn something quickly is still by doing it yourself. Being able to perform a task under the guidance and supervision of a mentor who performs the task first and then observes the learner undertaking the task and correcting them as necessary is a very efficient way of learning for the learner.

'However, one-on-one training is costly and unreliable, depending on the availability of a mentor, and in the long run: unsustainable. Also, it lacks the consistency vital in any business, especially in a franchise that succeeds by implementing consistency across the network. So, there's no standardisation because you're dependent on the one team member/mentor who happens to be available in the franchise at that time. Replicate this across a 20-, 200- or 2000-store network, and this becomes a significant drawback. That's when even this peer-to-peer training becomes hugely inefficient.

'So, you need to go for a digital alternative, and that's where we come in. We try to get as close as we can to that person-to-person on-the-job training environment. People want to learn by watching their peers perform a task. This is today's preferred and ideal way of learning. Even traditional eLearning zones and their instructions are too far away from this, so they are not fit for purpose.

'We optimise this whole flow of knowledge dramatically, starting with the digitisation of sharing and learning.

'Take onboarding, critical employee engagement that defines, creates, and promotes culture – essential in a franchise because you can tell a great deal about a business by the way that it welcomes new team members. The aim is to make the new starter feel welcome so they can complete their job to your standards, feel comfortable in their new role and hit the ground running.

'In your Patisserie Pénélope case study, an experienced baker might need to learn how to create a PowerPoint presentation to create instructions for a recipe. Even if they know how, designing the information and fitting it to the pages takes time. And frankly, their motivation is low because they're not sure it will be used.'

'This is a hugely inefficient process,' Jorim concludes. 'You want to make it easy, fast and engaging, because those things drive efficiency – and that's what you will need in a changing workforce. So, what we've designed, what we've done with Manual.to, is to optimise each of those components in the process.'

Complex techniques and procedures

Pastry chefs create a wide range of pastries and baked goods. Many of these require complex techniques and procedures. For visual learners who may struggle to understand these procedures through written instructions alone, videos are an invaluable tool for improving their skills and performance. Here are some ways that video is used to support visual learning for pastry chefs:

- **Recipe demonstrations:** The patisserie creates videos demonstrating how to prepare specific recipes. These videos show the step-by-step process, including techniques for mixing ingredients, shaping dough and decorating finished products. Visual learners benefit from seeing these procedures in action, which can help them understand the nuances of the recipe and improve their performance.

- **Equipment training:** The patisserie creates videos demonstrating how to use various pieces of equipment such as mixers, ovens and pastry bags. These videos show the equipment's correct setup, operation and maintenance, which helps visual learners perform these tasks more effectively.

- **Customer service:** The patisserie creates videos demonstrating how to interact with customers and deliver the perfect customer experience. These videos show techniques for greeting customers, recommending products, upselling and handling complaints. Visual learners can benefit from seeing these procedures in action, which can help them deliver improved customer service.

Using video in these ways, the patisserie provides learners with a more engaging and practical learning experience. This can help improve the quality of the products, reduce waste and errors and enhance customer satisfaction.

Smartphone recording

Filming workplace instructions/procedures on a smartphone can take less time than creating written instructions, enabling the franchisor to develop the Operations Manual more quickly and effectively. It may take a little practice, but in no time, creators can achieve great results.

In our fictional Patisserie Pénélope case study, team members are encouraged – and challenged – to find innovative ways of working as part of the franchisor's quality management system. If taken up and shared with the network, this becomes best practice.

The assistant manager, Mary, uses her smartphone to make a video snippet for each of the thirty stages of the butter softening process starring her colleague, Sam, the kitchen hand. Mary makes sure not to record Sam's face or any identifying characteristics. This is important because, should it become necessary to update a video snippet, this can be done seamlessly. It also helps avoid issues when employees leave the company.

In our case study, shooting thirty video snippets for the butter softening instruction took Mary 45 minutes, with only one retake using her smartphone. Mary and Sam don't need to write and memorise a script because they won't be adding a voiceover. They'll add texts in Manual.to – a web-based platform for creating multilingual video plus text instructions.

Uploading video snippets and adding a short text

Mary must now upload her video snippets and add captions for each of them. The captions can then be read or converted into speech. Artificial Intelligence (AI) can also translate them into commonly used languages:

- She logs in with her username and password to access the knowledge-sharing platform.

- She uses the web-based editor to add a new document in the 'Day-to-Day Operating Requirements: Kitchen' section.

- She types in the title and uploads an image of a pat of butter to represent the instruction.

- She uploads the first video snippet and then types the text for the caption.

- She repeats the process for the following twenty-nine video snippets.

- She reviews the butter softening instruction.

- When satisfied with the result, she asks her manager to review and approve it.

- When approved, her manager contacts Patisserie Pénélope's business development manager.

- He makes a final review of each video snippet and caption.

- Any minor edits are made before publishing the instruction. (The instruction can still be edited after publishing.)

- After publishing the instruction, the business development manager clicks 'share' and the new instruction is made instantly available to the entire network.

- There's an option to download and share a unique QR code or to share the unique URL. This takes just seconds. Franchisees can then print the QR code and place it where needed in minutes.

- They connect the label printer to print off one or more labels.

- The QR code with the butter softening QR code label is then placed near the microwave in the bakery kitchen.

Reading the QR code

Rémy joined the expanding Ermington patisserie last week as a second kitchen hand. When he arrives for work, one of his tasks is to remove the butter from the fridge to ensure that it's sufficiently soft for baking. Today, he forgot! Flustered, he tells his boss, the pastry chef. 'Don't worry, we've all done that,' his boss says empathetically. 'We have the answer.'

His boss takes Rémy to the microwave and shows him the QR code. Rémy's relieved. He understands the significance of the QR codes posted throughout Patisserie Pénélope from induction training the week before.

- Rémy takes his smartphone, opens the camera app and captures the QR code.

- This takes him to the butter-softening procedure instantly.

- Here, he chooses to listen to the text in his native French, because texts can be converted into speech and translated into the most-used languages using AI.

- Rémy completes the thirty simple steps.

- The butter is softened perfectly. Voilà!

QR codes provide 'how-to' procedures at the point of need, when needed. No faffing around finding the relevant page in a hard copy manual or locating the instruction in the digital edition in the cloud.

Planning shots

Now let's look at planning the shots you want to capture. This will help you avoid missing critical steps and ensure you have all the video snippets you need to create clear and comprehensive work instructions.

EXAMPLE: Workwear and personal hygiene

1. Employees must be well-groomed and maintain a neat and professional appearance to reflect the company's brand and values. (Shots to represent each key role.)

2. Appropriate workwear with our logo must be clean, well-pressed and in good repair. (Focus on the traditional baker's uniform; show how this must/must not be worn.)

3. Staff handling and preparing unwrapped food must put on a clean apron or tabard over their clothes. (Shot of clean apron or tabard.)

4. A badge with your first name must be worn on the left-hand side. (Show the location of the name badge.)

5. Comfortable black shoes must be worn. (Focus on different types of shoes worn for different roles/never trainers.)

6. Long hair must be neatly tied back. (Customer-facing staff shot from the side.)

7. Bakery staff must use a hairnet, especially when handling unwrapped food. If hair is not tied back or

covered, it is more likely to fall into food, and staff are more likely to touch their hair. ('Amusing' shot of horrified 'customer' finding a long black hair in a Victoria sponge.)

8. Clean, short fingernails are essential for maintaining hygiene standards. (Focus on hands with clean, unvarnished, trimmed nails.)

9. Only one plain wedding band. No other jewellery such as earrings are permitted. ('Amusing' shot of team member trying to extract an earring from a bowl of mixture.)

10. Jewellery must be removed and secured in your locker on arrival. (Shot of team member securing jewellery in their locker.)

11. Staff must not smoke, drink, eat or chew gum while handling food. (Shot of staff member eating while prepping or serving customers. Add a red X across the image.)

12. Staff must avoid touching their face or nose, coughing and/or sneezing over or near food, and wash their hands if they do. (Shot of kitchen hand sneezing into a bowl.) Add handwashing sequence.

EXAMPLE: Disposal of waste

1. Dispose of waste properly. (Shot of designated wastebin/s.)

2. Dispose of all used cleaning supplies and paper towels in the designated bin. (Shot of waste being dropped into the designated wastebin.)

Summary

- As attention spans shorten, franchise team members increasingly prefer quick, easy-to-digest content.

- Video can be used to provide a rich and engaging learning experience.

- Video can be particularly effective for complex or technical procedures.

- Many franchisees benefit from visual rather than text-based instructions, particularly those involving complex processes, equipment or procedures.

- How you create a video will vary according to whether you add it to a knowledge-sharing centre or platform.

- Plan the shots you want to capture to help you avoid missing critical steps.

PART THREE
DRAFTING TO PUBLICATION: THE ICING ON THE CAKE

Crafting great content is like baking a batch of cookies. Just as baking cookies requires careful attention to detail (measuring ingredients, setting the oven temperature and monitoring the baking time), writing great content requires attention to detail (grammar, punctuation and formatting) to ensure a polished, professional end product.

10
Elements Of A Good Draft

Imagine walking into Patisserie Pénélope. The wafting aromas of fresh pastries and warm bread lure you in, making you feel welcome and intrigued. That's exactly what your franchise Operations Manual should be like – inviting, engaging and filled with easily digestible information.

We've all been in bakeries where the bread is hard as stone and impenetrable and the pastries unappealingly dense. That's a metaphor for the labyrinthine, overly formal writing style that has dominated operations manuals for far too long. You bite into it and you're immediately lost in a maze of jargon, struggling to make sense of the information.

It's time to replace the hard loaves and heavy pastries with light, flaky croissants and melt-in-your-mouth pastries – to break free from the corporate jargon and embrace clarity and human connection.

Over the past 35 years, I've been through countless bakeries and seen all kinds of bread and pastries – or in this case, Operations Manuals. It's clear that the best ones are those with the human touch, where you can taste the care and attention that went into baking each piece.

Your Core Operating Brand Standards Manual (COBSM) should be the same. It should be a 'good read' that utilises clear, concise language, just like a perfectly baked baguette is simple, yet immensely satisfying. Avoiding the pitfalls of overly formal and impersonal writing is like avoiding overbaked and flavourless bread – it makes for a much more enjoyable experience.

A relatable and engaging writing style is the icing on the cakes, making them more appealing and memorable. This accessible writing style, much like an easy-to-eat pastry, will empower your franchisees to quickly grasp and apply the information in the manual and its library of tools and resources, savouring the taste and coming back for more. This will ultimately lead to their success and satisfaction – and a thriving, bustling patisserie that everyone loves to visit.

By the end of this chapter, you will:

- Know how you can transform your COBSM into a valuable resource that speaks to your franchisees in a language they understand and appreciate.

- Learn what else you can do to make your manual clear, concise and engaging.

- Use your smartphone camera to capture the *Manual Magic* Resource Centre QR code to access additional Tools & Resources.

Structure & Contents template

You or your team of expert content providers identified in the Project Plan will now need to create content from the Structure & Contents template created in Chapter 3 and the five initial headings and SOPs discussed in Chapter 7, Underpinning The Franchise Agreement:

1. **Review the Structure & Contents:** You / they should start writing content by first thoroughly reviewing the Structure & Contents to understand the context of their allocated Section / s.

2. **Gather existing material:** If any existing material or resources related to the Topics in the outline are available, gather them. This could include

existing training materials, policy documents, Standard Operating Procedures or other related materials – eg, Tools & Resources. See Chapter 3.

3. **Brainstorm additional information:** For each Section and Topic in the Structure & Contents template, brainstorm and make a list of additional information, examples or details that should be included to make the manual as comprehensive and helpful as possible.

4. **Write the first draft:** Start writing the content according to the Section/s allocated in the Project Plan. Use clear, concise language and make sure to cover all the topics listed in the structure. Keep the language consistent and make sure the information is easy to understand.

5. **Use real-life scenarios:** To make the manual more engaging and practical, include real-life scenarios or examples wherever possible. These can help franchisees understand how to apply the information in a real-world context.

6. **Review and refine:** Once the first draft for a section is complete, review it for clarity, accuracy and completeness. Look for areas that could be misunderstood or need more detail. Make sure the information flows well and is logically organised.

7. **Incorporate visual elements:** Consider incorporating diagrams, flowcharts, infographics or images to break up the text and enhance

understanding. These can be especially helpful for complex processes or procedures.

8. **Get feedback:** Ask a trusted colleague or advisor to review the draft. They may spot areas of confusion or suggest areas that need more detail. Use their feedback to refine and improve the manual.

9. **Revise and proofread:** Based on the feedback, revise the content. Then, proofread for grammar, punctuation and spelling errors. This is also a good time to ensure that the manual's formatting is consistent throughout.

10. **Repeat the process:** Repeat this process for each Section of the manual until the first draft of the entire manual is complete.

11. **Review for legal and compliance:** Before finalising, it's essential to review the manual to ensure all statements, policies and procedures are compliant with applicable laws and regulations.

This process, though time-consuming, will ensure that the Core Operating Brand Standards Manual is thorough, clear and valuable to franchisees. Bear in mind that a good draft is a work in progress. The first draft of your Operations Manual can be pretty dreadful, but if you're not an experienced writer or a professional editor, it can be hard to know what elements make your draft informative, readable, and relatable – and what needs improvement or revision.

Communicating your purpose

Ask yourself: What is my purpose? The more specific this purpose is, the better. Knowing *why* you're writing something is essential, so that you can think about how best to communicate with your target audience.

Your purpose will vary according to your audience. If your target audience is franchisees with little or no management experience operating within a single territory, the way you communicate information will differ from that of an experienced master franchisee/brand partner that already operates several businesses/franchises successfully, has a dedicated management team in place to develop a region or country (approved by you) – and has well-developed systems in place for all businesses.

If the former, you will need to spell out – 'Janet and John' style[14] – everything the franchisee and their team member(s) need to know to replicate each part of your Business System faithfully. This is a style of writing that uses simple, straightforward language where the sentences are short, the words are easy to understand, and the story is told in simple steps, as a child might write. It's also called 'the plain style' in academic circles.

---

14 The term 'Janet and John style' comes from the original 'Janet and John' book series written by Rona Munro, which were used by parents in the 1950s and 1960s to teach their children how to read.

If master franchisees/brand partners are your target audience, you can accept that they know what it takes to operate a Business System – but not *your* Business System. Although it may be broadly similar, you must communicate how they will do things 'your way' and provide guiding principles to ensure that these percolate from management to newly appointed franchisees for the duration of the franchise term.

Important considerations

- Make sure your draft is readable, using simple language and avoiding jargon. You want your franchisees to understand the information in your manual, so it needs to be written for them – not for you or someone else who works at head office.

- Ensure that all the information is organised logically and clearly so that readers can easily find what they need, when needed. This will help readers find information quickly, which is essential since they will likely read your manual when confused or stressed.

- Ensure that every bit of content has a goal and a reason for being there. If there's no reason for it to be included – if it doesn't serve any purpose – remove it!

- Your structure should be logical and clear. It should also allow your reader to follow your argument or argumentation easily.

- Use headings, subheadings and bullets to help organise your thoughts into a coherent whole.

Mandatory obligations

A friendly tone must be balanced with the mandatory obligations of the contractual relationship and the steps that *must* be followed to meet the franchisor's operating and brand standards. Using Patisserie Pénélope as an example.

EXAMPLE: Mandatory obligations

You *must*:

- Operate your patisserie in accordance with local employment laws and any other legal requirements, including the franchise agreement.

- Recruit to clearly defined job descriptions and roles and ensure adequate training is provided to every team member, so they know what is expected from them and can be confident in the delivery of their role.

- Recruit sufficient staff to meet the operational capacity planning requirements to deliver customer service to meet our quality standards.

- Make all applicants aware of the career progression opportunities available through the different training and development programmes.

- Minimise staff turnover to maintain stable teams consistently delivering superior customer service – the Patisserie Pénélope way – to every customer.

- Comply with Patisserie Pénélope's data protection policy.

Optional requirements

While following best practice may be considered optional, as a franchisor, you will want to strongly recommend that your franchisees follow best practice procedures.

EXAMPLE: Optional requirements

- Successful businesses are based on a sensible, well-constructed business plan, which *we strongly recommend* you monitor (every month) and adjust when necessary.

- You should review your progress against your business plan each month. The sooner you identify a positive or negative trend, the faster you can take advantage of it – or deal with the problem without harming the future of your business.

- It is helpful to set out key factors to check (monthly), which will indicate the health of your business. These will include the impact of sales during specific promotional periods or the average profit per order.

- As a rule, you should conduct a performance review every month in relation to:
  - Sales/margins/net profits
  - Sales development
  - Work management
  - Performance compared with your business plan (key indicators)
  - Key Performance Indicators
  - Self-management

Your brand's authentic voice

Incorporating your brand's authentic voice into the franchise Operations Manual creates a strong foundation for franchisees to understand and implement the brand's values, culture and operational standards. This ensures a consistent experience for customers across all franchise locations and contributes to the brand's overall success. Representing your brand's authentic voice is one of the key differentiators between an unhelpful Operations Manual and one that will help your franchisees succeed.

A brand's authentic voice refers to its unique, consistent, genuine tone and style in communicating with its audience. This voice reflects the brand's personality, values and mission and helps create a strong connection with customers by fostering trust and loyalty. An authentic voice distinguishes a brand from its competitors, making it recognisable and memorable.

An authentic brand voice is a powerful tool for building lasting customer relationships by being consistent,
honest, relatable, emotionally engaging and adaptable. It's a voice reflecting the brand's essence and
allowing it to stand out.

Critical elements

Critical elements of a brand's authentic voice are:

- **Consistency:** Maintaining a consistent voice
  across all communication channels such as
  social media, advertising and customer service
  is crucial for a strong brand identity. This
  consistency helps build customer trust and
  creates a cohesive brand image.

- **Honesty and transparency:** An authentic brand
  voice is open and honest, even when addressing
  shortcomings or mistakes. Being transparent
  about company practices, decisions and values
  makes customers feel more connected to
  the brand.

- **Relatability:** An authentic voice should
  resonate with the target audience using
  language, references and experiences they can
  relate to. This creates a sense of camaraderie
  and understanding between the brand and
  its customers.

- **Emotional connection:** A brand's authentic voice
  should evoke emotions in its audience, whether

happiness, inspiration or a sense of belonging. This emotional connection fosters brand loyalty and creates a deeper, more meaningful relationship with customers.

- **Storytelling:** Include stories and real-life examples from the brand's history or successful franchise locations to illustrate best practices and convey key messages. This makes the content more engaging and strengthens the brand's voice. It helps franchisees better understand and connect with the brand.

- Sharing the brand's story (as in our fictional Patisserie Pénélope case study), including its history, mission and values, through a compelling narrative helps humanise the brand and makes it more memorable. Storytelling is a powerful tool for creating an emotional connection with the audience.

- **Adaptability:** While maintaining consistency is essential, a brand's authentic voice should be flexible enough to adapt to changing trends, customer needs and cultural contexts. Being able to evolve while staying true to the brand's core values demonstrates authenticity and resilience.

Brand identity ensures consistency

Incorporating your brand's authentic voice across all elements of the KSE is essential for ensuring consistency and a strong brand identity across all franchise locations.

1. Consistent language and tone

Use consistent language and tone throughout to reflect your brand's voice. This includes using the appropriate level of formality and your brand's unique phrases, and maintaining a consistent writing style that aligns with the brand's personality.

The Core Operating Brand Standards Manual is the key document that serves as a guide for your franchisees to follow in operating their businesses, so it should be written in a friendly tone, using language that is easy to read and understand.

How we write can influence readers' thoughts and feelings about what they're reading. Some people prefer a more formal tone, while others are more comfortable with a casual approach. It's essential to keep your tone light and friendly. Your writing style should be warm and welcoming so that the reader feels like they can't wait to read more. Using first-person helps build rapport with your readers, making them feel more connected with you as their franchisor and more invested in what you have to say. Here are some tips for writing in a friendly tone:

- Use contractions (I'm, you're, he's).

- Use 'you' instead of 'one' or 'the franchisee'.

- Use 'we' frequently instead of 'the Company' or 'the franchisor'.

- Avoid jargon.

Begin the manual with an Introduction encapsulating the brand's story, mission and values. This sets the tone for the rest of the manual and reminds franchisees of the core principles that guide the brand.

2. Visual elements

Incorporate the brand's visual identity into the manual page layout and multimedia elements, such as the logo, colour scheme and typography. This creates a cohesive look and feel that reflects the brand's image and reinforces its identity.

3. Brand values and culture

Emphasise the brand's values and culture. This can be done by sharing examples of how these values are exemplified in daily operations, providing case studies or offering practical tips on embodying the brand's culture.

4. Clear and concise communication

Ensure the content is well-organised, easy to understand and concise. This makes it more accessible for

ELEMENTS OF A GOOD DRAFT

franchisees and reflects the brand's commitment to professionalism and efficiency.

5. Franchisee input

Provide opportunities for franchisees' feedback and encourage them to share their experiences, suggestions and/or feedback. This fosters community and collaboration and helps keep the brand's voice authentic and relevant.

Plan updates

Operations Manuals are the foundation of all franchise systems. A franchise is all about the system, so it's what a franchisee pays for. Simon Bartholomew, the British Franchise Association's Chief Operations Officer (Operations), says,

> 'In my experience, manuals are soon outdated unless there is a comprehensive method of updating every page on a regular basis. As a franchisor, how can you expect a franchisee to follow your system if you don't keep them updated?
>
> 'Development and change is the strength of a franchise system, but it needs to be documented to ensure it encompasses the whole network.'

Keep the manual updated with the latest additions, changes, or modifications to your Business System – eg, brand developments, best practices and operational changes. This is the franchisor's obligation under the franchise agreement. It demonstrates the brand's adaptability and commitment to continuous improvement.

So, plan your updates – and stick to your plan. With today's technology, additions can be made in real time.

Authentic brand voice examples

These are some examples of a franchise brand's authentic voice. Each franchise brand showcases a distinct, authentic voice that reflects its unique values, offerings and target audience. By maintaining a consistent and genuine voice, these businesses effectively communicate their brand identity and create strong customer connections across all locations:

Costa Coffee

Costa Coffee, a UK-based coffee shop franchise, has an authentic voice emphasising quality, warmth and community. Their messaging often focuses on their commitment to using sustainably sourced coffee beans, providing a comfortable and welcoming environment, and fostering connections with local communities. Costa Coffee's voice is friendly, approachable and passionate about coffee and service excellence, resonating with customers who value great-tasting coffee and a welcoming atmosphere.

I worked with Costa Coffee between 2006 and 2009 to develop and subsequently update volumes for the Costa suite of Operational Manuals. We incorporated and consistently repeated in context the slogan: 'An Unbeatable Coffee Experience – great coffee, at speed and with a smile' throughout all the content. This continuously conveyed to Costa's brand partners and outlet managers that this was the minimum operating standard across the Costa 2000+ franchise global network for uniformity and consistency.

Costa had undertaken extensive customer research to establish what defines 'An Unbeatable Coffee Experience'. We then created a set of minimum operating standards based on their customer research results. These standards defined what Costa's customers wanted and would like to experience when they visited a Costa outlet in terms of product excellence, service and environment. These standards underpinned the Terms & Conditions of the franchise agreement. Research results were also the basis of the audit system we created.

For a more detailed insight into the development of their Operational Manual, their case study can be accessed by capturing the *Manual Magic Library* QR code from your smartphone or tablet camera.

manualmagic.manual.to/library

McDonald's

McDonald's was the first franchise created in the USA in the 1950s. A global fast-food franchise, it has an authentic voice focusing on consistency, affordability and convenience. Their messaging often highlights their commitment to serving familiar, high-quality food quickly and at reasonable prices.

McDonald's voice is friendly, approachable and inclusive, aiming to create a sense of community and catering to a diverse audience with varying tastes and preferences.

The Body Shop

The Body Shop, a British cosmetics and skincare brand, has an authentic voice emphasising ethical practices, sustainability and cruelty-free products. Their messaging revolves around their commitment to using natural, ethically sourced ingredients, fighting against animal testing and promoting environmental responsibility.

The Body Shop's voice is compassionate, empowering and environmentally conscious, resonating with customers who value ethical and eco-friendly personal care products.

Specsavers

Specsavers, a leading UK optical and hearing care franchise, has an authentic voice focusing on professionalism, value and exceptional customer care. Their messaging often emphasises their commitment to providing affordable, high-quality eyewear and hearing products and outstanding service tailored to individual needs.

Specsavers' voice is knowledgeable, trustworthy and caring, resonating with customers who value expert advice and personalised care in their optical and hearing services.

Writing voice

In business writing, the primary goal is to communicate information concisely and professionally. Several types of writing voice are used in business content, each suited to different contexts and purposes. The most appropriate type of writing voice for a given business document depends on the purpose, audience and context. When selecting the most suitable writing voice, the goal of the communication, the intended recipients and the company culture or industry standards all need to be considered.

As discussed in Part One, Chapter 3, Building Your Structure & Contents, there are several types of franchise structures:

- Single-unit franchise

- Multi-unit franchise

- Area development agreement

- Master franchise agreement

- Development agreement

- Joint venture franchise

You will need to use the voice most appropriate to the structure and the type of franchisee using your Operations Manual. If master franchisees/brand partners are your target audience, you can accept that they know what it takes to operate a Business System – but not your Business System. Although it may be broadly similar, you must communicate how they will do things 'your way' and provide guiding principles to ensure that these percolate from management to newly appointed franchisees. For example, when we communicated with Costa's brand partners, we pitched the voice and tone appropriate to how you would address senior executives responsible for developing a region or country. When we communicated with the AA Driving Instructors, we assumed little or no prior management experience.

The main types of writing voice are as follows.

1. Formal voice

A formal writing voice is characterised by precise language, proper grammar and adherence to standard writing conventions. It maintains a professional, objective tone and avoids colloquial expressions, contractions and slang. Formal writing often employs complex sentence structures, a passive voice and advanced vocabulary. This style is most appropriate for documents that require a high degree of professionalism such as contracts, legal documents, formal reports and official correspondence. Franchise examples include:

- Franchise agreements, an undertaking of confidentiality / non-disclosure, summaries of legislation and regulations, policies

- Employment contracts

- Business plans

- Letters of appointment, notices, agendas and minutes of meetings

2. Informal voice

Informal writing is more conversational and relaxed, using everyday language and a friendly tone. It allows for contractions, colloquialisms and personal pronouns, creating a more accessible and engaging text. Informal writing often uses shorter sentences and an active voice. It is well-suited for internal communications, casual emails, blog posts and social media updates.

3. Persuasive voice

The persuasive writing voice aims to convince the reader – your franchisee – to take a specific action or adopt a particular point of view. It employs rhetorical devices such as appeals to emotion, logic or credibility, and uses strong, action-oriented language. Persuasive writing may also address potential objections and emphasise the benefits of the proposed action or viewpoint. This style is most effective in sales pitches, marketing materials, business proposals and opinion pieces.

4. Instructional voice

Instructional writing focuses on providing clear, step-by-step instructions to guide the reader through a process or task. It uses simple, direct language and often employs an active voice, bullet points and numbered lists. The goal is to convey information in a concise, easy-to-follow manner. This style is commonly used in operations manuals, user manuals, Standard Operating Procedures, how-to guides and training materials.

The instructional voice is crucial in creating content for an Operations Manual. A well-crafted Operations Manual provides franchisees with clear, concise and easy-to-follow instructions on running the business per the franchisor's guidelines and expectations. This voice is also used for creating text-based content and video using captions and audio instructions. The instructional voice is characterised by:

- **Clarity:** Use simple, straightforward language that is easy to understand. Avoid jargon, technical terms or complex sentence structures that may confuse the reader.

- **Active voice:** Use the active voice to make the text more engaging and easier to follow. For example, write, 'Place the order' instead of, 'The order should be placed'.

- **Step-by-step guidance:** Break down tasks into individual steps, using numbered lists or bullet points to clearly outline each action required.

- **Visual aids:** Incorporate diagrams, flowcharts or images to represent processes and provide additional clarity visually.

- **Consistency:** Use consistent terminology and formatting throughout the manual to ensure continuity and ease of understanding.

5. Analytical voice

The analytical writing voice is used when presenting data, research findings or in-depth topic analysis. It requires critical thinking, logical reasoning and synthesising information from multiple sources. Analytical writing is clear, objective and evidence-based, using data and examples to support its conclusions. This style is appropriate for whitepapers, case studies, research reports and academic articles.

6. Descriptive voice

Descriptive writing paints a vivid picture using rich details and sensory language. It employs adjectives, adverbs and figurative language to create an engaging and evocative text. The goal is to help the reader visualise a person, place or object and to elicit an emotional response. Descriptive writing is often used in product descriptions, company profiles, travel or destination marketing and creative storytelling within a business context.

Remember that the most appropriate type of writing voice for a given business document depends on the purpose, audience, and context. It's essential to consider the goal of the communication, the intended recipients, and the company culture or industry standards when selecting the most suitable writing voice.

Write to be understood

The Operations Manual marks the start of the franchisor's relationship with the franchisee. Pay careful attention to the writing voice, as it sets the stage for the future. Here are some tips for writing voice in the Operations Manual from Anne Janzer, author of *Writing to Be Understood: What Works and Why*:[15]

- Write in a voice that is friendly, welcoming and clear – and that matches the overall franchise brand. For example, if the brand is about 'fun and family', write in a voice which reflects that to show the franchisee how it's done.

- Use personal pronouns (we, us, you, etc) instead of your company/brand name and franchisee/brand partner/master franchisee to set the relationship off on the right foot. You want your franchisees to see themselves as part of something more significant rather than someone receiving orders from on high.

- Save the legalese for legal documents and avoid industry-specific terminology. If you must use it then be sure to define it clearly, or create a

---

15   A Janzer, *Writing to Be Understood: What Works and Why* (Cuesta Park Consulting, 7 August 2018)

separate glossary of terms at the end of the Introduction to your Operations Manual.

- Try reading what you've written aloud to see how your voice 'sounds' to someone unfamiliar with your industry. If an eighth-grader can't understand it clearly, then rewrite it until they can. You can find online tools to assess the grade level of your writing.

Content consistency and coherence

As the editor-in-chief for the Costa Coffee Operational Manual and the AA Driving School Manual, each project manager reviewed all content for accuracy and completeness and then passed the content to me to edit for consistency in voice, tone and style and to correct any deviations from the desired voice.

I reviewed and edited all content against the Structure & Contents template and the franchise agreement. If necessary, I offered suggestions for improvement – eg, incomplete procedure or ambiguous meaning. Any business-specific terminology was added to the growing glossary.

If necessary, the project manager returned the piece to the content providers to complete or provide additional explanation. Otherwise, the edited content was held, ready for 'sign-off'.

There were times when the content providers needed help to articulate their expertise. My role was to coach, mentor and help them understand the context of the procedure. Often, we created their content together. It was essential that no one felt inadequate in the process, as each was an expert in their own field. I wasn't.

Ensuring that multiple expert content providers write in the same voice to maintain consistency and coherence in the final output is essential. Here are several strategies you can employ to achieve this goal:

- **Style guide:** Create a comprehensive style guide that outlines the desired writing voice, tone and style. Include guidelines on grammar, punctuation, formatting and any industry-specific terminology. Share this guide with all content providers to ensure they follow the same conventions.

- **Conduct training sessions:** Organise and conduct training sessions or workshops for the content providers where you discuss the desired writing voice and review the style guide. This helps to align everyone's understanding of the expectations and enables them to ask questions or seek clarification.

- **Provide examples:** Share examples of the desired writing voice with the content providers. This may include excerpts from previously published work or specially created samples demonstrating the preferred style and tone.

- **Monitor and adapt:** Continuously monitor the content produced by your content providers to ensure that the writing voice remains consistent over time. Be prepared to adapt the style guide or provide additional guidance as necessary.

- **Foster collaboration:** Encourage content providers to collaborate and share their work. This can help them learn from one another and understand the desired voice better.

- **Maintain open communication:** Establish an open line of communication with the content providers, allowing them to ask questions, seek feedback or discuss concerns related to the writing voice. This ensures they feel supported and empowered to stick to the desired style.

- **Celebrate successes:** Acknowledge and celebrate instances where content providers have effectively adopted and maintained the desired writing voice. This positive reinforcement can motivate them to continue producing high-quality, consistent content.

- **Conduct regular reviews:** Schedule periodic reviews with your content providers to discuss their progress and address any challenges they may face in adopting the desired writing voice. I met with the AA Driving School department heads every six weeks to review the status of the various components of the AA Driving School Instructor's Manual. We easily resolved any issues when providing content and editing the drafts. We had tight deadlines, which were mostly met. Their manual came in on time and within budget.

For more detailed insight into the development of AA Driving School's Operations Manual, their case study can be found at www.manual-writers.com/recommendations.

Checklist

Here's a checklist of important things to consider when writing content:

- **Write conversationally:** Use a friendly and approachable tone that mimics natural conversation. This will make the text more engaging and relatable to the reader.

- **Focus on the reader:** Address the reader directly, using 'you' and 'your' to create a personal connection and make the content feel relevant to their situation.

- **Use simple language:** Choose everyday words and phrases and avoid jargon or technical terms that may be confusing to readers.

- **Use a professional tone:** While maintaining a conversational style, ensure that the writing remains professional and respectful, avoiding slang or colloquial expressions.

- **Use clear, descriptive headings:** Make it easy for readers to scan and find the information they need with informative headings that accurately reflect the content of each section.

- **Start with a strong opening:** Grab the reader's attention with an interesting fact, question or statement at the beginning of each section or subsection.

- **Maintain a logical flow:** Organise content in a way that makes sense, guiding readers through a clear progression of ideas.

- **Provide clear, actionable advice:** Offer practical guidance and specific steps that readers can follow to achieve the desired outcome.

- **Use transitions effectively:** Smoothly connect ideas and sections by using appropriate transition words and phrases such as 'however', 'in addition' and 'for example'.

- **Be consistent with terminology:** Choose specific terms for key concepts and use them throughout your manual to avoid confusion.

- **Address potential objections:** Anticipate concerns or questions that readers may have and address them directly in the text.

- **Emphasise key points:** Use bold and italics to highlight important information and make it stand out from the rest of the text, but underline sparingly.

- **Vary sentence structure:** Mix short and long sentences to create a more dynamic reading experience and maintain the reader's interest.

- **Break up long paragraphs:** Divide lengthy paragraphs into shorter ones, using bullet points or numbered lists to make the content easier to read and digest.

- **Use storytelling techniques:** Incorporate anecdotes, examples and case studies to make the content more engaging and memorable.

- **Use analogies and metaphors:** Help readers grasp complex concepts by comparing them to familiar ideas or objects.

- **Incorporate quotes and testimonials:** Include quotes from successful franchisees or industry experts to add credibility and a human touch to your content.

- **Edit ruthlessly:** Review the text for clarity, conciseness and accuracy, eliminating any unnecessary words or phrases. Use the editor's adage: if in doubt, leave out!

- **Check for consistency:** Ensure that formatting, punctuation and capitalisation are consistent throughout your manual.

- **Proofread carefully:** Take the time to thoroughly proofread your manual, checking for grammar, spelling and punctuation errors. Ask a colleague or professional proof-reader to review the document for a fresh perspective.

Summary

- A well-crafted and cohesive writing voice reflects the brand's commitment to professionalism, quality and efficiency, setting the tone for your franchisees to follow in their daily operations.

- Incorporating the brand's authentic voice into your Operations Manual strengthens its identity, fostering a sense of unity and belonging among franchisees.

- Maintaining a consistent brand voice throughout your manual ensures franchisees understand and implement the brand's values, culture and operational standards uniformly across all locations.

- Using a relatable and engaging writing voice helps your franchisees better connect with the brand and its mission, making the content more impactful and memorable.

- An appropriate writing voice that is clear, concise and easy to understand ensures that your franchisees can quickly grasp and apply the information in the manual.

- Using storytelling and real-life examples in the manual helps create an emotional connection between your franchisees and the brand, fostering loyalty and commitment.

- To ensure that multiple expert content providers write in the same voice, an editor should:

  - Develop a comprehensive style guide, conduct training sessions and provide examples of the desired writing voice.

  - Encourage collaboration, maintain open communication and edit for consistency.

  - Schedule regular reviews, monitor and adapt as necessary, and celebrate successes to motivate content providers to maintain the desired voice, tone and style.

11
Finalising The Draft

Finalising the draft of your Core Operating Brand Standards Manual and its linked tools and resources should be like applying the finishing touches to a beautifully crafted cake. Just as you would carefully smooth the last layer of icing, add decorative fondant flowers, or sprinkle on glittering sugar crystals, finalising your Operations Manual requires the same meticulous attention to detail. You must ensure that every word and every instruction is in its rightful place, serving its purpose in the grand scheme of your knowledge-sharing environment.

This final stage is not about making substantial changes or adding new layers to the cake – rather, it's about perfecting what's already there, ensuring it's ready for presentation. You proofread for spelling, grammar and clarity, just like you'd inspect every inch of your cake for imperfections. You cross-check information to ensure consistency, just like you'd ensure each slice of cake is the same size, ensuring fairness and uniformity.

The finalisation process is your last opportunity to make your Operations Manual as polished and palatable as possible, just like adding that final swirl of frosting or that last sprinkle of powdered sugar on a cake. It's about turning something good into something truly exceptional, something that will not only serve its practical purpose but will also delight those who use it. After all, a cake is not just for eating, and an Operations Manual is not just for reading – they are both experiences to be enjoyed, savoured, and revisited time and again.

By the end of this chapter, you will:

- Understand the finalisation process.

- Learn what's involved in proofreading.

- Know when you need professional help.

- Use your smartphone camera to capture the *Manual Magic* Resource Centre QR code to access additional Tools & Resources.

Importance of a well-finalised draft

The Core Operating Brand Standards Manual (COBSM) is the core document that guides every franchisee to faithfully replicate your system. It represents your business, your values and your commitment to consistency and excellence. Its finalisation is not a mere formality, but a crucial step in building a reliable, effective and efficient franchise operation.

A well-finalised draft ensures that each franchisee has the necessary knowledge and guidance to run their outlet effectively, leading to higher performance across the franchise system. Lynne Lister, Director and Founder, X-Press Legal Services Ltd explains:

'Developing a set of Standard Operating Procedures to replicate the Business System in detail proved to be such a laborious and challenging job! Also, we weren't entirely confident that anyone would follow our system or manual processes. We didn't even know how a manual should be constructed – or the appropriate wording to use without causing confusion. Would it work if we used graphics to demonstrate our 'how-to' process? Of crucial importance, was the manual sufficiently professional to encourage people to join us in our franchise?

'If we had our time again, we would allocate a budget sufficient to hire a professional writer to document all our processes. This would be at the top of our priorities because it isn't feasible to operate and support a franchise without a well-structured, user-friendly Operations Manual.'

Understanding the finalisation process

Finalising your draft COBSM is not just about proofreading; it is an intensive process that demands a thorough review and refinement of the content. It requires a deep understanding of the franchise system, attention to detail and the ability to communicate complex information in a clear and concise manner. The finalisation process is the opportunity to ensure that the manual is a true reflection of your Business System, providing comprehensive, accurate and accessible information to your franchisees.

Preparing for finalisation

There are several important things you need to do to prepare your draft. Before embarking on the finalisation process, conduct a thorough review of the manual's content to ensure completeness and accuracy. You must ensure that:

- It covers all aspects of the franchise operations in detail – from setup to sale.

- Every piece of information is current and accurate, reflecting the latest developments in your Business System and the broader sector.

- It's a cohesive and unified guide. That means it shouldn't read like a collection of unrelated documents. It should have consistent formatting, language and tone throughout. A uniform manual looks and feels professional. It also enhances readability and comprehension, reducing the chance of misunderstandings or misinterpretations.

The art of proofreading

Proofreading is not simply about catching typographical errors; it's about ensuring that the manual is clear, concise and error-free. This is your last line of defence against any mistakes or inconsistencies that may have slipped through previous revisions. It's an opportunity to refine the language, eliminate redundancies and improve the overall readability of the manual. Here are some top tips for proofreading your Core Operating Brand Standards Manual draft:

- **Understand the audience:** Keep in mind who will be using the manual. The language should be clear, concise and easily understandable for franchisees and key team members. Avoid using overly technical jargon unless necessary.

- **Ensure consistency:** Be consistent with terminology, formatting and style throughout the document. This includes the use of fonts, colours and layout.

- **Check for completeness:** Make sure that all the necessary Topics are covered, including training, marketing, daily operations, reporting, health and safety guidelines, customer service and quality control. The manual should be comprehensive enough to guide a franchisee through all the aspects of running the franchise.

- **Review for accuracy:** The manual must be accurate in terms of the business model, operational details, legal compliance and financial management aspects. Check for inaccuracies or misleading information.

- **Focus on clarity:** The instructions should be precise and clear. Avoid ambiguity and make sure instructions are explicit.

- **Check legal and regulatory compliance:** Ensure that all the procedures and policies mentioned comply with your franchise agreement, local laws and regulations.

- **Break down complex information:** If the manual includes complex operations, break them down into smaller steps. It's easier to understand and follow.

- **Use graphics and visual aids:** Pictures, diagrams, flowcharts, and infographics can be helpful in explaining complex procedures where using multimedia isn't feasible.

- **Spell-check and grammar-check:** The goal here is to eliminate any misspelt words and grammatical errors which can undermine the credibility of your manual and lead to misunderstandings. Strategies for improving grammar and punctuation include:

  - If you're not sure about use of punctuation or a grammatical convention, consult online sources.

  - Learn effective proofreading strategies such as reading your document aloud to help you focus on each sentence individually to identify grammatical errors.

  - Use spell-check and grammar-check tools such as Grammarly Pro and ProWritingAid to catch any typographical or grammatical errors.

  - Use a thesaurus to find synonyms for overused words, to learn and use new words regularly and to pay attention to the language used in good-quality writing.

- **Use a second pair of eyes:** Once you have gone through the manual, ask someone else to read it as well. They might spot mistakes or areas of confusion that you missed.

- **Iterative review:** Review the document multiple times. It's easy to miss errors in the first pass.

- **Table of contents:** Make sure the manual is easy to navigate with a clear table of contents and fully searchable for quick reference.

- **Feedback from franchisees:** If possible, ask your pilot franchisees or franchisee panel to review the manual and provide feedback. They can offer valuable insights into what's clear and what's confusing.

- **Test procedures:** Where possible, test the procedures in the real world to ensure they work as intended.

Please note: While I have provided detailed information, there's even more that could be explored on these topics. For instance, enhancing word choice and vocabulary in writing could be an additional focus area. This involves choosing words that accurately convey your intended meaning and are appropriate for your audience.

Cross-checking for consistency

Cross-checking is the process of comparing different sections or elements of your Operations Manual – including all tools and resources – to ensure consistency and accuracy. This is crucial, because inconsistencies can confuse readers and lead to errors in the implementation of your Business System.

Uniformity goes beyond consistent formatting and terminology. It also means ensuring that all procedures, policies and key messages are applied consistently across all operational procedures. Review your manual to ensure that it provides clear and consistent instructions for all operations and scenarios.

To cross-check efficiently, consider creating a checklist to verify key information across all the different elements of your manual. This will include procedures, policies and brand standards. Using digital tools can also help to automate some aspects of this process and improve accuracy.

Updating

Remember that an operations manual is a living document. It must be updated regularly as procedures, tools and policies change. Establish a process for updating the manual and informing franchisees of updates.

Seeking professional help

Using a professional editor to edit your franchise Operations Manual can bring several advantages:

- **Clarity and precision:** Complex instructions and processes can easily be misunderstood if not explained clearly. A professional editor can help make these complex ideas more understandable by simplifying the language or breaking down complex sentences. They can ensure the instructions are precise, eliminating ambiguity. This can help prevent operational mistakes in your franchises.

- **Consistency:** Your manual needs to maintain a uniform tone, style and language to provide a coherent reading experience. Inconsistencies can cause confusion. A professional editor can ensure that all parts of the manual follow the same formatting rules and language usage. This includes consistent use of terminology, fonts, headings and more.

- **Grammar and spelling:** Even small spelling mistakes or grammatical errors can undermine the credibility of your manual. They can also cause misunderstandings. Editors are experts at spotting these errors and will help to ensure your manual is error-free.

- **Organisational structure:** A well-organised manual makes it easy for the reader to follow and understand the material. An editor can help organise the content logically and ensure there is a smooth flow of ideas. They can help with the creation of an intuitive table of contents, effective headings and subheadings, and appropriately labelled diagrams and charts.

- **Compliance:** There will be references to sector-specific regulations or standards in your Operations Manual. A professional editor with experience in franchising *and* your sector can help ensure your manual covers these requirements.

- **Saves time:** Editing a manual is a time-consuming process. It requires a meticulous review of each line and a deep understanding of the content to ensure accuracy. By hiring a professional editor, your team can focus on their areas of expertise like managing business operations or franchise relationships, while the editor takes care of refining the manual.

- **Professional presentation:** A well-edited manual comes across as professional and polished. This can enhance your franchise's image, showing that you pay attention to detail and strive for excellence. It gives potential franchisees more confidence in your brand, and it may even become a deciding factor for them when choosing between different franchise opportunities.

Summary

- Every word and every instruction must be in its rightful place, serving its purpose in the grand scheme of your Operations Manual.

- Proofreading is not simply about catching typographical errors; it's about ensuring that the manual is clear, concise, and error-free.

- A professional and polished manual enhances your image in the eyes of your current and future franchisees.

- An Operations Manual is a living document. Minor changes to procedures, policies and tools must be updated in real time. Major updates must be planned – and executed.

12
Production

Baking the perfect bread or creating the most delectable pastry isn't just about having the right ingredients. It's also about knowing how to mix them together, when to let them rest and how to bake them to perfection. Similarly, in the dynamic bakery of franchising, two essential ingredients are effective communication and access to critical resources. Without these, your franchise will be like a loaf of bread without yeast, unable to rise to its true potential.

In our modern world, the oven we need to bake our franchise to success is technological solutions. Just as Patisserie Pénélope would employ a high-tech oven with precise temperature control for perfect baking, franchisors should consider using cutting-edge technology to upload and distribute and share their knowledge. The Operations Manual can be likened to a secret bread recipe, detailing the steps each franchise must follow to create the same delicious product.

But it's not enough to just have the recipe. Everyone in the bakery must be able to access it and work with it. This is where our digital oven comes with another advantage. It makes the recipe easy to access and allows for collaboration among all the stakeholders. This is how pastry chefs work together in a kitchen, each adding their own, unique touch to the final product.

Now, not all ovens are the same, and the same applies to the platforms for uploading your Core Operating Brand Standards Manual (COBSM) and multimedia elements. This chapter, like a baker's guide to the best ovens, gives you an overview of various ways to share your knowledge, their key features, tools, resources – and potential drawbacks.

In franchising, it's essential to have a good grasp of the tools at your disposal and how to utilise them to achieve success. This is like baking, where having the right ingredients is equally important.

Ultimately, baking a successful franchise, like baking a delicious loaf of bread or a perfect pastry, is about using the right ingredients, the right tools and the right methods. To achieve this, franchisors must employ modern technological solutions. These enable you to upload and distribute your Operations Manual. They also facilitate easy access and collaboration among franchisees.

This will include guidance on creating a structured folder hierarchy, managing access controls, enabling versioning and collaboration and regularly updating the content to ensure franchisees have access to the most up-to-date information and resources.

By the end of this chapter, you will:

- Understand the importance of selecting the most appropriate methods to upload and manage your manual, considering factors such as ease of use, accessibility, security, collaboration capabilities and cost-effectiveness

- Learn about several popular ways to share your know-how and their unique features and benefits, and their suitability for different franchisor requirements

- Learn best practices for organising and managing the Operations Manual and other franchise-related materials on these platforms, following the now-familiar Category > Section > Topics > Tools & Resources hierarchy

- Use your smartphone camera to capture the *Manual Magic* Library QR code to access additional Tools & Resources

Cloud storage and collaboration platforms

Several cloud storage and collaboration platforms are available to upload a digital copy of an Operations Manual, together with Tools & Resources. Cloud storage and collaboration platforms are being continuously improved and upgraded. New ones will be introduced. An IT professional can help you evaluate the pros and cons of what's available. It should be aligned to your franchise network development strategy. Plan to review this quarterly to ensure that it continues to meet your needs for knowledge sharing.

When choosing to upload the elements of your Operations Manual, you should consider factors such as ease of use, storage capacity, security, appropriate access controls, collaboration features, access control and pricing. Depending on your specific needs and requirements, one platform may be more suitable than others.

They are perfect for organising and managing the Operations Manual and other materials, following the now familiar Category > Section > Topics > Tools & Resources hierarchy.

Below are two popular options, along with their advantages and disadvantages. I have used both Dropbox and Microsoft SharePoint to collaborate with clients to create and edit draft content. These franchisors have shared their Operations Manual with their networks prior to setting up an intranet/franchisee portal.

Dropbox

Dropbox is a popular cloud storage service that provides file synchronisation, personal cloud, and client software. It's often used for personal storage, but it also offers features that make it a practical solution for businesses looking to distribute and share documents, like an Operations Manual. Here's an overview of how Dropbox can serve as a cloud-based knowledge-sharing environment:

- **Document storage and synchronisation:** Dropbox's primary function is as a cloud storage platform, making it a suitable place to store and share an Operations Manual. The synchronisation feature ensures that all users see the most updated version of the files.

- **Collaboration:** Dropbox allows multiple users to collaborate on documents via Dropbox Paper, a collaborative workspace where teams can write, edit and coordinate together in real-time. Comments and feedback can be directly attached to the specific sections of the manual.

- **Permissions and security:** Dropbox provides control over who can access and edit files. Permissions can be set for individual users, ensuring that only authorised franchisees can access and make changes to the Operations Manual. Dropbox also has robust security features, including two-step verification and encryption of files both at rest and in transit.

- **Search:** Dropbox includes a search feature, which can be used to quickly locate documents or specific content within documents. This can help franchisees find the information they need from the Operations Manual quickly.

- **Accessibility:** As a cloud-based service, Dropbox can be accessed anywhere with an internet connection and on any device. This is important for franchise operations that are spread out over multiple locations and time zones.

- **Integration with other tools:** Dropbox integrates with a variety of other tools and platforms, including Microsoft Office and Google Workspace, allowing franchisees to work in the applications they're already familiar with.

- **Version history:** Dropbox keeps a history of all deleted and earlier versions of files, allowing users to restore files or revert to previous versions if necessary.

As with SharePoint, using Dropbox effectively may require some initial setup and user training, especially for those who are not familiar with the platform. Dropbox is generally more straightforward and user-friendly than SharePoint, but it lacks some of the advanced customisation and collaboration features that SharePoint offers.

Microsoft SharePoint

Microsoft SharePoint is a web-based collaborative platform that integrates with Microsoft Office. It's primarily used as a document management and storage system. It's highly configurable, and usage varies substantially among organisations. It's a powerful tool, requiring some technical skill to set up and manage effectively. Training may also be necessary for users who are unfamiliar with the platform.

When it comes to distributing an Operations Manual, SharePoint can serve as a cloud-based KSE in these ways:

- **Document management and storage:** The fundamental use of SharePoint is for storing, organising and locating documents, making it an ideal place for a text-heavy Operations Manual. Documents can be checked in and out, versioned (meaning you can track and manage edits), and even set to require approval before they're visible to all users.

- **Collaboration:** SharePoint provides an environment where stakeholders can collaborate on documents. They can co-author documents in real time, comment, and see changes as they are made. This makes it easy for franchisees to ask questions or provide feedback on the Operations Manual.

- **Permissions and security:** SharePoint has robust security and permissions settings. This means you can control who has access to the Operations Manual, who can edit it and who can only view it. This is important in a franchise environment where different levels of access may be required.

- **Search:** SharePoint's search functionality is powerful and can help franchisees quickly find what they're looking for in the Operations Manual. They can search for words within documents and even filter their search by author, date modified, and more.

- **Accessibility:** Being a cloud-based service, SharePoint can be accessed anywhere, anytime and on any device. This is ideal for a franchise operation where franchisees might be spread across different locations and time zones.

- **Integration with other tools:** SharePoint integrates seamlessly with other Microsoft Office products, making it easy for franchisees to work on documents in familiar applications like Word, Excel or PowerPoint.

- **Customisation and scalability:** SharePoint is highly customisable and scalable. You can build custom sites, add or remove features and scale up or down as your franchise operation grows.

A franchisee portal/intranet

This is the concept of a franchisee portal/intranet and how an Operations Manual can be uploaded. This is where different types of database materials can be uploaded so that they can be accessed by franchisees. These are the main features:

- **Secure login:** Franchisees should be provided with unique usernames and passwords to access the portal or intranet. This secure login system ensures that only authorised users can access the platform and its resources, protecting sensitive information from unauthorised access. This may involve implementing multi-factor authentication (MFA) for an added layer of security, as well as periodic password resets and account lockouts after multiple failed login attempts to protect against potential security breaches.

- **Customisable access:** The franchisor should have the ability to manage and customise access permissions for different users within the franchisee portal. This ensures that franchisees only have access to the resources and tools relevant to their specific roles and responsibilities. Customisable access can be achieved through Role-Based Access Control (RBAC), which assigns permissions based on predefined roles and responsibilities within the franchise system. This approach not only enhances security by limiting access to sensitive information but also streamlines the user experience by presenting franchisees with the most relevant resources for their specific needs.

- **User-friendly interface:** The franchisee portal should have an intuitive, easy-to-navigate interface with clear menus, categories, and labels for organising different content and resources. This interface should be accessible on various devices, such as desktops, laptops, tablets, and smartphones, ensuring franchisees can access the platform anytime, anywhere. A well-designed interface enhances user experience, making it easier for franchisees to find and access the information they need quickly and efficiently.

- **Operations Manual upload:** The franchisor should be able to upload the Operations Manual to a designated section of the portal in a user-friendly format, such as a PDF or an interactive web-based document. This section should be easily accessible from the main dashboard or navigation menu and organised into chapters or sections for easy browsing and reference. The Operations Manual should also be searchable, allowing franchisees to locate specific information or topics as needed quickly.

- **Database materials upload:** The portal should include designated folders for database materials following the Category > Section > Topics > Tools & Resources hierarchy. The Sections under these key Categories should be organised in a logical, hierarchical structure, making it easy for franchisees to navigate and find the needed materials. The platform should also support various file formats, such as text documents, images, videos, or spreadsheets, to accommodate the diverse range of resources that franchisees may require.

- **Support and training resources:** The portal should include a dedicated section for support resources, such as FAQs, video tutorials, and troubleshooting guides, to assist franchisees with using the platform and addressing common issues or concerns. In addition, the portal should provide access to training materials, such as online courses, webinars, or training manuals, to help franchisees enhance their skills, knowledge, and understanding of the franchise system.

- **Version control and updates:** The portal should have version control features to ensure that franchisees always have access to the most up-to-date materials, including the Operations Manual. This may involve automatic syncing, version tracking, and archiving previous versions for reference. Franchisees should receive notifications about updates, either via email or through the portal itself, to keep them informed about changes to the resources they rely on.

- **Collaboration and communication tools:** The franchisee portal should include discussion forums, group messaging, and file sharing to facilitate communication and collaboration between franchisees and franchisees and the franchisor. These tools can help foster community and support within the franchise network, enabling franchisees to share best practices, ask questions, and discuss challenges. Integration with popular communication platforms like email, instant messaging, or video conferencing tools can further enhance collaboration capabilities.

- **Analytics and reporting:** Franchisees should have access to performance reports and data specific to their operations and benchmarking data from the broader franchise network. This can help franchisees monitor their performance, identify areas for improvement, and make data-driven decisions to enhance their business operations. The portal should provide visualisation tools like graphs, charts, or dashboards to help franchisees easily interpret and analyse the data.

- **Feedback and improvement mechanisms:** The franchisee portal should include features that allow franchisees to provide feedback on the resources, tools, and overall experience of using the platform. This can be achieved through surveys, comment sections, or dedicated feedback channels. By regularly collecting and analysing this feedback, the franchisor can identify areas for improvement, address any issues or concerns, and refine the portal to support the needs of the franchisees better. This collaborative approach can also strengthen the relationship between the franchisor and franchisees, fostering a culture of continuous improvement and shared success within the franchise network. Additionally, these feedback mechanisms can provide valuable insights into the franchisees' needs, helping the franchisor develop new resources or training programmes to address emerging challenges or opportunities.

Knowledge-sharing centre

A knowledge-sharing centre is a platform or facility that promotes exchanging information, ideas, experiences and expertise among individuals, organisations or communities. These are the main features:

- **Accessible content:** A knowledge-sharing centre should have a user-friendly interface with an advanced search feature, allowing users to quickly locate resources by keyword, category or other filters. The resources should be curated by experts or AI algorithms to maintain quality and relevance. Regular updates should be made to ensure that the content is up-to-date and reflects the latest advancements in various fields. Multilingual support and content translation features can also be beneficial in making the centre more inclusive and accessible to a global audience.

- **Collaboration tools:** The collaboration tools in a knowledge-sharing centre should be versatile and support various types of interaction such as real-time chats, asynchronous discussions, file sharing and project management. These tools should be available across different devices and platforms, allowing users to collaborate effectively regardless of location or preferred device. Integration with popular productivity and communication tools can also facilitate seamless collaboration and information exchange.

- **User-generated content:** To foster user engagement and community-building, the knowledge-sharing centre should provide intuitive tools to create, edit and share content in various formats such as text, images, videos or presentations. A peer review or moderation system can help maintain the quality of user-generated content, while recognition and reward mechanisms such as badges, points or leaderboards can incentivise users to contribute valuable content and expertise.

- **Personalisation and customisation:** A knowledge-sharing centre should use AI-driven algorithms to analyse user behaviour, preferences and interests to provide tailored content recommendations, learning paths or expert connections. Customisable dashboards and user interfaces allow users to adjust the layout, themes or widgets to suit their preferences and working styles. Users should also control their notification settings, allowing them to receive updates and alerts based on their interests and priorities.

- **Networking opportunities:** To facilitate professional networking, a knowledge-sharing centre should provide features such as searchable user directories, profiles highlighting user expertise and achievements and tools for connecting with peers or mentors. Users should be able to join or create interest-based groups, communities or virtual events that provide opportunities for networking, learning and collaboration.

- **Integration with external systems:** A knowledge-sharing centre should offer seamless integration with external data sources like open access repositories, government databases or industry-specific resources. This can broaden the scope of available knowledge and enable users to access up-to-date and accurate information. Integration with other software tools or platforms such as learning management systems, project management tools or social media platforms can enhance the user experience and streamline workflows.

- **Analytics and reporting:** Advanced analytics and reporting tools should be available to provide users with insights into their learning progress, content consumption patterns and knowledge-sharing impact. For organisations, these features can help track employee engagement, identify knowledge gaps and inform decision-making for training and development initiatives. Visualisation tools like charts, graphs or heatmaps can help users and administrators better understand and interpret the data.

- **Accessibility and user-friendliness:** The knowledge-sharing centre should be designed using accessibility best practices such as responsive design, keyboard navigation and compatibility with assistive technologies like screen readers. Clear and concise language, along with tooltips or contextual help, can guide users through the platform. A dedicated help centre or support resources such as tutorials, FAQs or webinars can further enhance usability and user satisfaction.

- **Security and privacy:** The knowledge-sharing centre should implement industry-standard security measures such as secure socket layer (SSL) encryption, data-at-rest encryption and MFA. Regular security audits, vulnerability assessments and updates should be conducted to identify and address potential risks. The platform should also adhere to relevant data privacy regulations and provide users with clear information about data collection, usage and storage policies.

- **Continuous improvement and support:** A dedicated team should be responsible for the ongoing maintenance and enhancement of the knowledge-sharing centre. This includes monitoring user feedback, conducting user experience testing and refining features based on insights gained. The team should also provide user support through various channels such as email, phone, chat or helpdesk systems to address questions or concerns in a timely manner. Regular training sessions, webinars or workshops can be organised to help users make the most of the platform and stay updated with new features or best practices. By continually refining the platform and engaging with the user community, a knowledge-sharing centre can remain relevant, effective and valuable to its users.

Knowledge-sharing platform

The rapid expansion of a franchise network comes with its own set of challenges, one of which is the efficient dissemination of information, resources and best practices across the entire network. With a growing number of franchisees, it becomes increasingly important for a franchisor to maintain a streamlined communication system that fosters a culture of collaboration and innovation. In such cases, upgrading a knowledge-sharing centre into a knowledge-sharing platform such as Manual.to can prove to be an invaluable decision, offering numerous benefits to both franchisors and franchisees.

A knowledge-sharing platform is a digital or online tool that facilitates the efficient exchange of information, ideas and resources among individuals within an organisation. These platforms are built using software, web applications or cloud-based services, enabling users to access and share information from any device with internet connectivity. This stands in contrast to traditional knowledge-sharing centres, which are physical or virtual spaces primarily focused on promoting learning and skill development through the exchange of knowledge, experiences and best practices.

When a franchise network expands to include, say, thirty franchisees, upgrading to a knowledge-sharing platform can offer several advantages:

- **Efficient information dissemination:** As the number of franchisees grows, it becomes increasingly challenging to ensure that everyone has access to the most up-to-date information and resources. A knowledge-sharing platform allows franchisors to easily distribute and update important documents such as the Core Operating Brand Standards Manual, marketing materials and training resources, ensuring that all members have access to the latest content.

- **Fostering collaboration and innovation:** A knowledge-sharing platform provides a centralised space for sharing ideas, insights and expertise. This can help foster a culture of collaboration and innovation within the franchise network, enabling franchisees to learn from each other's experiences, share best practices and work together to overcome common challenges.

- **Centralised resource management:** As a franchise network grows, it becomes increasingly difficult to manage and organise the wealth of information and resources available. A knowledge-sharing platform allows franchisors to maintain a single, easily accessible repository of knowledge and resources, reducing information silos and duplication of effort.

- **Scalability and accessibility:** Knowledge-sharing platforms can scale to accommodate growing organisations, ensuring that the platform remains functional and efficient as the franchise network expands. Additionally, their web-based nature ensures that users can access information and collaborate from anywhere with an internet connection, making it easier for franchisees to stay connected and informed, regardless of their geographical location.

- **Cost-effectiveness:** Implementing a knowledge-sharing platform can also be more cost-effective than maintaining a physical knowledge-sharing centre, as it eliminates the need for dedicated facilities and resources. This can free up valuable resources for the franchisor to invest in other aspects of their business such as marketing, training or product development.

In conclusion, upgrading a knowledge-sharing centre into a knowledge-sharing platform can significantly enhance the efficiency and effectiveness of communication and collaboration within a growing franchise network. By providing a centralised, accessible and scalable solution for information exchange and resource management, a knowledge-sharing platform can help franchisors and franchisees alike to thrive in an increasingly competitive business environment.

E-learning system

An e-learning system offers numerous benefits to franchisors. By leveraging technology to deliver educational content, e-learning systems can improve the training experience for franchisees and employees, making it more engaging, efficient, and accessible. Here are some key benefits of implementing an e-learning system:

- **Flexibility and accessibility:** E-learning systems enable learners to access training materials at their own pace, on their preferred devices, and from any location with internet access. This flexibility allows individuals to learn when it is most convenient for them, making it easier to fit training into their busy schedules.

- **Consistency:** E-learning ensures consistent training content and delivery across the entire franchise network. All learners receive the same information, presented in the same way, ensuring that everyone has a uniform understanding of the organisation's policies, procedures and best practices.

- **Cost-effectiveness:** By eliminating the need for printed materials, travel and on-site instructors, e-learning systems can significantly reduce training costs. In addition, e-learning materials can be easily updated, reducing the expenses associated with reprinting and redistributing outdated materials.

- **Scalability:** E-learning systems can easily accommodate the growth of the franchise network, as new franchisees and employees can be granted access to the training materials with minimal effort. This scalability ensures that training remains efficient and cost-effective as the organisation expands.

- **Customisation and personalisation:** E-learning systems can be tailored to meet the specific needs of individual learners, providing personalised learning paths and allowing learners to focus on the areas where they need the most support.

- **Interactive and engaging:** E-learning often incorporates multimedia elements such as videos, animations and interactive quizzes, making the training experience more engaging and enjoyable for learners. This increased engagement can lead to improved information retention and better learning outcomes.

- **Tracking and reporting:** E-learning systems often include analytics and reporting tools that enable organisations to track learners' progress, identify knowledge gaps and assess the effectiveness of training materials. This data can be used to make informed decisions about training content and delivery, ultimately improving the overall quality of training.

- **Creation and uploading:** As for the creation and uploading of content, this process typically involves several parties:

  - Subject matter experts: These individuals are responsible for providing accurate and relevant information on specific topics, ensuring that the training content is aligned with the organisation's policies, procedures and best practices.

  - Instructional designers: These professionals work with subject matter experts to design engaging and effective e-learning courses,

incorporating multimedia elements,
interactivity and assessments to enhance the
learning experience.

- Franchise corporate team: The franchisor's
corporate team often plays a role in reviewing
and approving the training content, ensuring
that it aligns with the brand's standards
and values.

- e-Learning administrators: These individuals
are responsible for uploading the content to
the e-learning system, managing user access
and monitoring the system's performance.

By leveraging the expertise of these various stakeholders, an e-learning system can deliver high-quality,
engaging and effective training that supports the
growth and success of the franchise network. Kate
Chastey MCIM, Franchisor of The Passionate PA (UK)
Ltd, says:

> 'I franchised my business officially in 2016
> when I launched my first "proper" franchise.
> Before that, however, I had a pilot franchisee
> who was pivotal to the success of my
> Operations Manual creation. Unlike most big
> and ambitious franchises, all my development
> was undertaken on a shoestring. I didn't have
> a Penny Hopkinson in my life… Goodness,
> I didn't even know such a fountain of all
> knowledge existed!

'So, I wrote my own Operations Manual. One page at a time. I did that with my pilot franchisee in operation. She didn't have the beautifully crafted, interactive platform we have today – she had me on speed dial, and every time she asked a question, I answered her and then wrote it all down.

'Slowly, very slowly, we created the first draft of the Operations Manual. It worked, however. In 2016-2018 I successfully launched three franchisees with that manual version. That first edition was in paper format. It required all training to be done face-to-face, and after initial training was complete, most franchisees closed the folder, put it on a shelf above their desk and got on with the job.

'We have a very different way of working today. After numerous updates and revisions, 2021 saw me move our entire Operations Manual online. We now have a user-friendly, super e-learning platform with massive scope for making the interface entirely our own.

'Each new franchisee receives a personalised training schedule which includes self-led training on the e-learning platform where there are videos, checklists, activities, etc. Plus, strategic masterclasses with me, face to face, on critical topics.

'Franchisees now revisit the Operations Manual frequently because it's easy, engaging and quick. It's still written in the same style as back in 2015 – fun, friendly and full of personality – but it's now more accessible.

'What I love most about the innovation of moving the manual online is how I can monitor what franchisees have reviewed and what they go back to at different points in their franchise term. This is invaluable when supporting them and helping them each be super successful.

'I regularly update the Operations Manual with content and amendments highlighted to the team in our monthly meetings. We also use the manual as a basis for learning in our monthly team meetings, keeping even the seasoned franchisees connected with this all-important document.

'As much as each of my franchisees is unique, what matters to all franchises is that the service and quality across the network are consistent. At The Passionate PA, we have a culture of excellence, and I genuinely believe this starts with the Operations Manual. New franchisees often comment on how well-written, engaging and thought-provoking the manual is. This same diligence and care must be demonstrated in the work they deliver to clients throughout their business. Our manual serves to set that standard of excellence for us all.'

Summary

- Cloud-based platforms offer remote storage, retrieval and sharing of information and resources, making knowledge accessible from any device with internet access, promoting collaboration and flexibility.

- A Knowledge Management Centre (KMC) is a centralised system that organises, stores and facilitates access to organisational knowledge, including documents, policies and best practices, ensuring consistent operations and decision-making.

- Knowledge-sharing platforms are online spaces designed to foster collaboration and knowledge exchange among users such as forums, social networks and wikis, encouraging collective learning and innovation.

- E-learning systems are digital learning environments that deliver educational content through multimedia, interactive modules, enabling learners to access training materials at their own pace and from any location.

Conclusion

Like any good recipe, you can always improve on the original. The Operations Manual should be considered a work in progress and focus on continuous improvement.

Many franchisors still rely on traditional, text-heavy hard copy or online manuals. These are not engaging and fail to capture the attention of franchisees. Usually, these manuals contain vast amounts of written information that can be difficult for franchisees to process, leading to confusion and a lack of implementation. To maximise the benefits of your Operations Manual, it's essential to move away from this outdated approach and create a dynamic resource that engages your franchisees and motivates them to apply the comprehensive procedures provided. Matthew Levington, Co-Founder, Business Doctors confirms this:

'When we first launched the Business Doctors Franchise back in 2008, having utilised an industry professional to help construct and write our manual, it followed the traditional approach of one big, fat ring binder and several smaller "programme leaders" guides, with more detailed explanations around each element of a business.

'While this worked wonders in terms of documenting each process within our business model, providing a fantastic point of reference both during training and beyond for the franchisees, it was a bit of a monster to both handle and navigate around. We also found it very time-consuming to issue updates every time you needed to upgrade or amend a particular process or accommodate external factors affecting the normal run of business. These would often get missed or even ignored by the franchisees, who were too busy running the businesses to deal with the admin.

'With the advancements in digital technology and communications, you will no longer find a ring binder in sight! We have adopted an online digital sharing platform, which we call Remedy, which contains all the best practice elements linked to the operation of our business, along with the associated training, modules, videos and online learning packages. This is not only more dynamic and easier for franchise partners to access and explore, but it also creates immediacy around the updates and internal communications. It also means that we can have a fully transparent two-way communication/feedback loop between the central support team at the franchise partners on the front line.

'It is absolutely critical that the franchisor maintains a "live" Operations Manual which can pivot and align with the ever-changing market conditions. This was, of course, put to the test during the Covid pandemic, where we had to completely reinvent how, as a business, we both engaged the market, and delivered our services.'

The demographics of today's workforce show that an increasing percentage of the workforce are Millennials. Their preference for non-traditional learning styles has led to significant changes in the workplace environment and the adoption of new ways of working and learning. Today's franchisees and their teams expect more from their Operations Manual. New and mature franchisors should now consider creating a dynamic and engaging knowledge-sharing environment because:

- **It encourages active learning:** A dynamic and engaging KSE encourages franchisees to take a proactive approach to learning. This fosters a culture of continuous learning, which is essential in today's fast-paced business environment.

- **It promotes understanding:** A KSE promotes understanding by presenting information in different formats. Franchisees and their teams can watch videos, read articles and participate in online discussions, all of which enhance their comprehension and retention.

- **It attracts and retains talented franchisees:** A dynamic and engaging KSE is an appealing feature for potential franchisees. It also helps existing franchisees feel valued and connected, which can improve their retention rates.

- **It enhances operational efficiency:** A KSE can help franchisees work more efficiently by providing training and resources on best practices, new technologies and industry trends.

- **It promotes consistency:** A comprehensive KSE ensures consistency across a franchise system, minimising the risk of errors and inconsistencies.

- **It encourages innovation:** A dynamic and engaging KSE can inspire franchisees to innovate and think outside the box. This can lead to new ideas and initiatives that benefit the entire franchise system.

- **It improves communication:** A KSE provides a centralised platform for sharing information and promoting communication between franchisors and franchisees.

- **It aligns with modern learning preferences:** A dynamic and engaging KSE aligns with modern learning preferences, which favour interactive and immersive learning experiences over traditional, text-heavy materials.

- **It promotes brand consistency:** A KSE can help ensure that all franchise locations adhere to the same brand standards and values, enhancing overall brand consistency.

- **It supports ongoing development:** A KSE supports ongoing development and continuous improvement, which is essential in a competitive and constantly evolving business landscape.

- **It caters to the modern workforce's learning styles:** This ensures that your manual drives franchisee success and strengthens your franchise system.

By providing them with a KSE and incorporating multimedia elements such as videos, graphics, and interactive tools, you can transform your manual into an indispensable Operations Manual that your franchisees will value and use actively.

This shift to knowledge sharing based on a multimedia approach enhances the user experience. It also improves the effectiveness of your manual in driving success and profitability.

Resources

U se your smartphone camera to capture the *Man-ual Magic* Library QR code for access to more Tools & Resources to help you with your Operations Manual. The resources will be continuously improved and updated.

These are just some of the many resources available. It's important to do your own research and due diligence to find the resources that best fit your needs and goals.

- The World Franchise Council (WFC) www. worldfranchisecouncil.org

- British Franchise Association (bfa) www. thebfa.org

- National Franchise Exhibition www.thenec.co.uk/whats-on/national-franchise-exhibition

- International Franchise Association (IFA) www.franchise.org

- International Franchise Convention www.franchise.org/convention

- Encouraging Women into Franchising (EWIF) www.ewif.org

Franchise publications

- Franchise World www.franchiseworld.co.uk

- Which Franchise www.whichfranchise.com/running-a-franchise

- Elite Franchise Magazine http://elitefranchisemagazine.co.uk

- Business Franchise Magazine www.businessfranchise.com

- Franchise Journal www.franchisejournal.com

- Global Franchise www.global-franchise.com

- Franchise Times www.franchisetimes.com

- Franchising Magazine USA https://franchisingmagazineusa.com

- Canadian Business Franchise Magazine www.franchiseinfo.ca

- Business Franchise Australia & New Zealand
  www.businessfranchiseaustralia.com.au

Books on franchising

These books provide valuable information and guidance on the franchising industry, including how to select a franchise, the legal requirements and responsibilities of franchisees and the key factors for success in franchising:

John Pratt, a UK-based lawyer, has written several books on franchising, including *The Franchisor's Handbook: Your Duties, Responsibilities and Liabilities* (About Face Publishing, January 2006) – the only legal textbook on franchising in the UK. Other titles of his include:

- *Practical Commercial Precedents* – Franchising chapter

- Contributor to American Bar Association Forum on Franchising (ABA): *Fundamentals of International Franchising*

- *Fundamentals of Franchising*

- Co-Editor of American Bar Association Forum on Franchising: *Fundamentals of Franchising, Europe*

Contributor to:

- UK Chapter 'Getting the Deal Through' – Common Law and Civil Law on Franchising Issues, available at www. lexology.com/gtdt/guides/franchise/ common-law-and-civil-law-on-franchising-issues.

- JURIS, Centre for International Legal Studies, Chapter on 'England' – International Franchising, Editor Dennis Campbell, www.jurispub.com/ England-International-Franchising-2nd-Edition. html.

- The International Distribution Institute (IDI) – Country Report – United Kingdom. Reports can be accessed on IDI's website, www.idiproject. com/documents-reports; you will need a membership to access them.

Carl Reader, a UK-based author, entrepreneur and academic, has written several books on franchising, including *The Franchising Handbook: How to Choose, Start and Run a Successful Franchise* (John Murray Learning, 14 July 2016)

Rune Sovndahl, co-founder and CEO of Fantastic Services, author of *Fantastic Business: Start, scale and succeed, learning from masters in franchising* (Rethink Press, 28 June 2022)

Franchising from Both Sides of the Fence, eBook (*Franchise World*, 2023), www.franchiseworld.co.uk/ franchising-from-both-sides-of-the-fence-ebook

Further resources

R Kaplan and D Norton, *The Balanced Scorecard: Translating strategy into action* (HBR Press, April 1996)

'Total Quality Management (TQM): A Complete Guide' (GoCardless, January 2023), https://gocardless.com/ guides/posts/what-is-total-quality-management-TQM

'What are some strategies for improving my grammar and punctuation?' (University of Louisville, no date), https://louisville.edu/writingcenter/for-students-1/ common-writing-questions-1/i-am-having-trouble-with-grammar-and-punctuation

'RV Franching Market Size, Share, Growth & COVID-19 Impact Analysis, Segmented by Type, Product, Application and by Geography and Forecast 2023–2030' (Market Reports World, March 2023), www.marketreportsworld.com/TOC/23106547#TOC

Acknowledgements

I would like to thank all my friends in franchising and the wider community who share my passion and have brought valuable insights. In particular, Pip Wilkins QFP, CEO, British Franchise Association, Joanna Dawson, Former International Operational Systems Manager, Costa Coffee (retired), Mark Peacock, Former Head, AA & BSM Driving Schools, Gill Balshaw, Head of Training Academy, the AA (retired), Penny Brooks, Training Manager, the AA (retired), and Jorim Rademaker, Founder and CEO, Manual.to.

I'm indebted to these colleagues who have contributed to my research and provided quotes or case histories. In particular, Simon Bartholomew, COO (Operations), British Franchise Association, Kate Chastey MCIM, CEO, The Passionate PA (UK) Ltd, David Costello

ACIB CeRCC VFP, Luke Frey, CEO, Bella Vista Executive Advisors, Anne Janzen, Author, *Writing to be Understood: What Works and Why*, Matthew Levington, Co-Founder, Business Doctors Ltd, Lynne Lister, MD, X-Press Legal Services, Susie McCafferty QFP, CEO, Platinum Wave Franchising, Jo Middleton, Franchise Mentor, Nina Moran-Watson, British Franchise Association Affiliate Solicitor, Nick Strong, MD, SocialHANDLER.

Special mentions also go to Geri England, Executive & Story Coach, Positive Change Workz, Dan Janal and members of his US WordStars Mastermind Group for their invaluable collective wisdom.

Not least, of course, I would like to thank my husband, Steven Bruce, who thought I was writing the Dead Sea Scrolls and has supported me throughout with unfailing encouragement and copious cups of coffee.

The Author

Penny Hopkinson's background is in journalism as a trade and specialist journalist, international editor, Middle East socio-economics correspondent, and quality management correspondent. She launched Manual Writers International® in 1986 to bring a fresh perspective to the operations manuals needed to underpin quality management systems for organisations that didn't need BS5750 (ISO9001) accreditation. Developing the Underwriting Agents Procedures Manual for the Corporation of Lloyd's proved the concept. Her 40-year love affair with franchising took off in 1989 when she joined the British

Franchise Association as an affiliate professional advisor, having developed operations manuals for three franchisors. In 2011, she was appointed a Companion of the BFA in recognition of an outstanding personal contribution to the development of franchising in the UK. Her experience working with franchisors and franchisees in almost every sector has provided unique insights into the challenges faced by both parties and the power of a well-crafted Operations Manual that evolves with the times. Her latest book, *Manual Magic: Create the Operations Manual Your Franchisees Need to Succeed*, shows franchisors how they can create engaging operations manuals that underpin the franchise agreement and help their franchisees succeed.

For more information, visit my website:

🌐 www.manual-writers.com

Join me on social media at:

in Linkedin.com/in/pennyhopkinson

🐦 @manualwriters

📷 @manualmagic1